PHILIP M. STERN

GEORGE de VINCENT

The Shame
of a Nation

with a Foreword by

Vice President

HUBERT H. HUMPHREY

Ivan Obolensky, Inc. New York

LIBRARY OF CONGRESS CARD NO. 65-20805
FIRST EDITION

There is no fiction in this book. Everything in it is real.

This includes the captions, all of which are words actually spoken by "dispossessed" Americans, although not necessarily by the person in the accompanying photograph.

Sources for all facts and statistics may be found on pages 173-180.

All of the incidents in the chapter, *The Samaritan as Cop* are real. Some of the practices described contravene the officially stated policies or regulations of welfare departments, but are nevertheless tolerated by them.

Book Design by Stefan Salter

Typography by Accurate Typesetting, Inc.

Printed by Scranton Lithographers

Bound by Economy Bookbinding Corp.

This book is dedicated to
Shelley and Leni

and also to the American Samaritans
who are devoting their lives
to working with and among the poor

many of whom opened the door—and our eyes—
to the life and lot of the American poor.

foreword

by Vice-President Hubert H. Humphrey

THE War against Poverty, to which President Johnson has called us, is one of the most urgent endeavors in which America is engaged.

To win this war will require not only the exercise of governmental leadership, but also the willing dedication of millions of men and women, aroused by the pity and shame of the poverty of America, and determined to engage themselves in a great national effort.

The stark and shocking facts of life among the poor in too many parts of America were brought home to the average American in the Thirties by the compelling art of the photographer and journalist. Through the cameras of Margaret Bourke-White, Dorothea Lange, Carl Mydans, Walker Evans, Arthur Rothstein, Ben Shahn and others, as well as through the reportorial eyes of such men as James Agee, John Steinbeck and Erskine Caldwell, many Americans found their consciences aroused and their emotions engaged.

"The Shame of A Nation" is in that strong photo-journalistic tradition. And it is perhaps even more important than its predecessors of the Thirties. For the Poverty of the Sixties, unlike the poverty of the Great Depression, is tucked away, off the main thoroughfares —largely out of sight. In the preparation of this book, the author, Philip Stern, and the photographer, George de Vincent, have left the highways, the well-traveled thoroughfares, and have penetrated the wall that circumstance has built between affluent America and impoverished America.

In "The Shame of A Nation," therefore, you will see conditions you may not have dreamed existed in this wealthiest of nations. You will meet some of America's neglected citizens, face to face. You will learn something of their lives, their environments, their problems, their needs, and the lot accorded them by this affluent society.

The pages you will see in this book are not reassuring. Many of the pictures are not pleasant to look at. One may disagree at times with the authors' conclusions. But one cannot ignore the bitter facts that their words and pictures reveal. Nor should those facts be ignored.

I would hope that every thinking American who opens this book would be stirred not only to shock and pity, but also to a powerful determination that such conditions must not be permitted to continue.

I would hope that one who sees these pictures would be challenged by them to search his mind and heart, and to ask, "What can I personally do about these conditions?"

What indeed, can we do about these conditions? We have begun a massive assault on the condition of poverty in America. We are dedicating huge human and financial resources to the struggle. But the problem of poverty far outstrips what government will be able to muster. What is needed, is courage, ingenuity, dedication—and the kind of understanding and insight you will, I believe, gain from "The Shame of A Nation." We need in short, the harnessing of the intellectual energies and economic power of private enterprise, of labor, of all the great voluntary organizations of America.

We can afford it. We have the wealth, the energy, yes, and the daring and imagination to defeat poverty in America, to relegate to the history books the sad and somber portraits of this volume.

Hubert H Humphrey

contents

introduction

"... poverty we think it no disgrace to acknowledge, but a real degradation to make no effort to overcome."

—*Pericles' Funeral Oration.*

In the year nineteen hundred and sixty-four, in the richest nation in the world—

—children in the capital of that nation went to school without breakfast; some vomited from sheer malnutrition.

—families in West Virginia were forced to a choice: shoes for their children, or food.

—six hundred people in New York and four hundred in Washington, D. C.—half of them under ten—were bitten by rats in slum tenements.

—a family of twelve in the nation's capital, unable to find a low-rent house that would accept nine children, lived—and spent Christmas—in a basement furnace room.

—near Phoenix, Arizona, a mother, father and seven children shoehorned themselves into a single 10 by 10 room, without toilet or running water.

—on a North Dakota Indian reservation, a one-room tar paper shack was too small for two parents and seven children, so some of them slept in wheelless, derelict cars outdoors.

—children in Mississippi under the aid-to-dependent-children program were given less than thirty-two cents a day to live on.

—the food allowance for large welfare families in the nation's capital came to seventeen and a half cents per person per meal.

All this in the year nineteen hundred and sixty-four. All this in the richest nation in the world.

Visitors to this land of plenty find this shocking. And so it is.

But the shock, the shame, lies not so much in the not-new *fact* of poverty amid plenty as in the manner in which an increasingly affluent society has forsaken its poor: ignored or excluded them, lost sight of their needs.

Somehow, the poor always seem to end up last—last not only in material wealth, but last to receive the rights and guarantees enjoyed by others, last to have their needs and problems attended to. Aid to starving Appalachia, aid for the aged sick, aid to migrant farm workers, a broader minimum wage—all these remained, in the year nineteen hundred and sixty-four, on the list of unfinished business.

Visitors to this land of abundance may wonder about its sense of priorities. It spends, for example, more for the care of migrant birds than for the care of migrant humans. It spends billions for highways for the two-car family, but less than a tenth as much to provide decent housing for the no-car family trapped in a slum basement. Billions for dredging rivers and harbors or for new military camps whisk through Congress, while sixty-year-old schools remain in overcrowded use, with no replacement in sight. Millions or tens or even hundreds of millions in tax and shipping and farm subsidies for the well-to-do; seventeen and a half cents per person per meal food allowance to welfare recipients in the capital of the richest nation in the world. *That* is the real shame of the nation.

Many Americans find comfort in the recollection that thirty years ago this nation did address itself to those needs. Laws were passed to aid the aged, the jobless, the low-paid, the helpless: social security, unemployment insurance, minimum wage, welfare. But many may not realize (or acknowledge) that these measures do not form an all-covering blanket. On the contrary, those who most urgently need these laws—the lowest paid, the most-often jobless— are still denied the warmth of their protection. Migrant bean pickers in Florida make a thousand dollars a year; cotton choppers in South Carolina get two or three dollars for a ten-hour day. Both are untouched by the minimum wage law.

Even for those covered, the blanket is often tenuously thin. The average jobless benefit, in the year nineteen hundred and sixty-four: thirty-five dollars a week (for a family of five, just one dollar per person per day). Average social security benefit for a couple, in the year nineteen hundred and sixty-four: twenty-nine dollars a week.

All Americans know that this land of plenty offers every child a free education. Free—but for some, virtually worthless. Many Americans may not be aware of what a survey found in a South Chicago slum: that although ninety-five out of a hundred had finished more than five *years* of schooling, more than half could not read or write well enough to do fifth-grade work.

Most Americans know that Congress has authorized a program for building low-rent public housing to provide decent shelter for the poor. Many may not realize that only a small fraction of that program has become a reality; that public housing accommodations are scarcest for the largest families—those for whom private housing is most desperately lacking—and that for many, it will take four, five or six more *years* of living in basement squalor before a public housing vacancy will open up. Even if present government goals are fulfilled, public housing will offer a refuge from squalor for only one slum family in eighty.

Most Americans know that billions are spent each year for welfare. Many may not be aware that some of these billions are being used to subsidize the illegal slum squalor in which many welfare "clients" live and for which the public pays the rent; or that some of the welfare billions are used to tempt fathers to desert their families (welfare aid often is withheld so long as the father remains with his family). Most important, many Americans may not realize that welfare workers usually spend more time policing and punishing, rather than helping and teaching; and that the welfare billions, as now spent, are not buying a way out of poverty and dependency. They are buying, instead, a virtual guarantee that today's generation of dependents will produce yet another generation on the dole in years to come.

3

Many Americans tend to look upon the poor with scorn, or with anger, or even with pity—but rarely with *understanding*. They bemoan the cost of poverty: the mounting accounts payable for social security or welfare or jobless benefits. They curse the consequences of poverty: violence, crime, illegitimacy, delinquency. Usually missing, however, is one crucial word: Why. *Why* more violence, more crime? (Is it really due to police or judicial laxity? Or is it due to the growing frustrations and tensions with which many humans must live?) *Why* more illegitimacy? (Is this pure immorality? Is it a willfully chosen path to larger handouts? Or is it due, in part, to society's failure to teach the means of avoiding unwanted children?) *Why* growing welfare rolls? (Is this the symptom of sheer shiftlessness? Or is it in part due to society's failure to remedy the mal-education that lies behind the welfare rolls?)

This may seem to be a book about the poor. But it is really much more about the rest of America and how it has viewed and treated the poor. *The Shame of A Nation* does not purport to examine all aspects of poverty or to offer any magic new answers. There are none.

This book grew out of a joint conviction on the part of both author and photographer that not only America's poverty, but her past "efforts to overcome it" deserve to be looked at with candor. Her poor deserve to be looked at with understanding. But the greatest imperative is that attention be paid to povetry's children. For without such attention, without heroic efforts to rescue them from ignorance and squalor, they will be the poor of tomorrow, the burden of tomorrow, the shame of tomorrow.

the dispossessed

A MIGRANT mother and her four children spend the winter in Florida in a tin shack: hot and steamy when the sun beats down; cold and damp when the sun is gone.

Her name: Esther Cook. Occupation: bean picker. Pay: sixty cents a hamper. A good day's picking: ten two-bushel hampers. That is, a good day means six dollars. But if the pickings are slim, a day's work may bring two dollars and a half or three dollars, maybe four. If it rains, no picking and no pay.

Her work week: seven days. Weekends, she is joined by her children. The older two work. The baby crawls up and down the rows.

In late spring the children quit school and, with twelve dollars to show for their winter's work, the family climbs into an ancient, long-retired school bus and starts "on the season." All one night they travel and all the next day and the next night. At the end of the journey: a migrant camp of porous wooden shacks, easy prey to a penetrating rainstorm. After two nights and a day on the bus, wet mattresses, wet floors, broken window panes, maybe covered by cardboard, maybe not. A stenchful, suffocating latrine. Flies buzzing around the washing-bathing spigots.

Out of the bus and back to the bean field. Sixty cents a hamper.

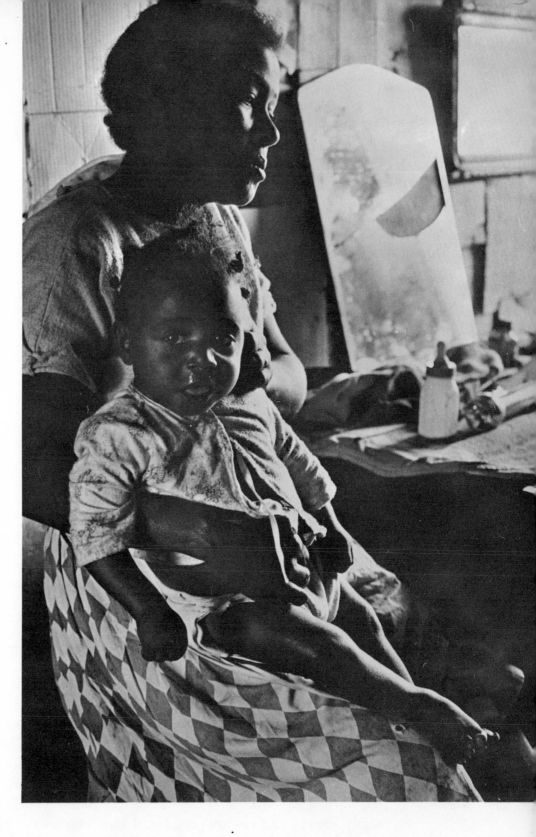

When she works in the fields, the baby crawls up and down in the rows.

*... Sixty cents
a hamper ...*

Fifty years ago, the first child labor law was passed. An issue was disposed of—or so it was thought.

A half century has elapsed, yet the problem persists. A half century has elapsed—yet to the children of this and other migrant mothers, the child labor law doesn't exist, for its protection is denied them. Half a million children—more than all the children of three Western states—still work in the fields. Many are injured there. A study showed that twenty per cent of farm injuries in California were to working children under sixteen.

Twenty-five years ago another law was passed, establishing a national minimum wage and stipulating that anyone working more than eight hours a day or forty hours a week was entitled to premium pay. A quarter of a century has passed, yet the migrant mother and others like her have yet to feel the warmth of that law's protection. Let her work ten hours a day or twelve; six days a week or seven—and it's still sixty cents a hamper. Let a man or woman chop cotton all day under the hot South Carolina sun—and it's two dollars or maybe three for the day's work. Thirty cents an hour. One fourth the national minimum wage.

Now the migrant mother of whom we speak is a native-born American citizen. For her, no minimum wage, no minimum transportation or sanitation. Those guarantees are denied to the native-

A migrant mother can't stop working just because she's pregnant.

9

born citizen—but not to the *non*citizens working in the next field: Jamaicans and Bahamians imported under contracts insisted on by *their* governments and enforced by roving liaison officers. There are no liaison officers to keep watch over the welfare of the migrant mother, a citizen of the richest nation in the world.

Why does she not band together with her fellow migrants to object to her second-class citizenship, to protest the importation of this wage-depressing competition? Here, too, she is handicapped. The law, now nearly two decades old, that protects other workers' right to organize into a labor union and bargain collectively still does not apply to her or to the other farm workers of America.

A migrant mother can't stop working just because she's pregnant. Her children must be fed every day of every week. So she, like other women who work at her side, has labored for her sixty cents a hamper even while a new and unwanted child grew within her. On the road, she has been hard pressed to get hospital help in

"When you work for fifty-sixty cents an hour, you ain't workin' and you ain't slavin'. You just givin'."

10

bearing her child, for she is no resident of the community. Of course, if she has a miscarriage, the ambulance will come to take her: a miscarriage is classified as an accident.

In a typical year, this migrant mother works just a hundred and nine days—which is to say she is unemployed about half the time. The plight of an industrial worker thus idled is cushioned by government payments, supplemented, if he belongs to a strong union, by employer payments under the union contract. But this migrant mother belongs to no union, and the unemployment compensation laws, enacted nearly three decades ago, do not exist for her.

The United States statutes also contain a law compensating workers injured or killed on the job. Most workers. Not all. Farm work is a comparatively dangerous occupation (accident rate third highest). Yet if the migrant mother or her children are injured in the fields, they receive not a penny. For this law, like the others, does not apply to them.

. . . mother and father both in the fields . . .

For the children of this and other migrant mothers, the child labor law doesn't exist.

"I made fifty cents today. I got somethin' to eat tonight. But tomorrow, I ain't got nothin' to eat."

"We works from can to can't for three-four dollars a day."

At the end of the journey, a migrant camp . . .

The migrants are not alone. Others are excluded from the protection of the nation's laws. The injury-compensation law excludes one out of five workers; out of 69 million workers in the U.S., only 29 million are covered by the minimum wage law; unemployment compensation does not exist for one worker in every three.

They are America's dispossessed.

Why are America's poor excluded from the mainstream of national progress?

Not because they are a minority; not because they constitute

. . . of porous wooden shacks, easy prey to a penetrating rain storm.

"I'd do better in the jungle than I do here."

only one-fifth of the population. The Negroes—numbering but one-tenth of the population—have found their voice. They have proven you don't have to be many to be heard.

The poor are dispossessed because they act singly and suffer singly, because they are voiceless; political impotents.

Because society has turned its face from them, the poor are not seen. Because they are voiceless, they are not heard.

But they are there.

the exiles

A FOUR-ROOM shack clinging precariously to the side of a hill near Hazard, Kentucky. Inside: a family of ten—the Darell Graveses.

Total family income: twenty dollars a month. Ten goes for rent. The other ten buys food stamps the government provides to keep families like this from starving.

This, plus Alma Graves' genius at inventing stomach-filling meals ("vinegar pie" is one of her specialties) keeps the family going—after a fashion.

For most of the children, no shoes. For all of the children, no doctor. If they get sick, Alma Graves "doctors" them herself (for instance, to keep eight-year-old Ronny from getting the convulsions that come with his high fevers, she lets him run around naked 'til his fever goes down). Months go by without Alma ever leaving that shack and going into town.

Darell hasn't worked in a couple of years. His trade is coal mining, but he has long since been replaced by a machine. His occupation now—or, rather, his preoccupation—is keeping ten people alive on twenty dollars a month.

Forty-five miles away, another shack, hard by a railroad track. Inside, Ray Newton and his family of five. Two beds and a crib for the six of them (the crib is shared by Sandra Lou, age eight, and

We abused our people. But when technology came, we replaced them first.

Jo Ann, age two). The only other furniture: a coal stove and a stick chair. The only reading material: the newspapers that seal walls and ceilings against the weather.

Family income: highly uncertain from one week to the next. If the truck mine needs Ray two days in a week, there's twenty dollars to keep six people alive; if there's only one day's work, only ten dollars.

Often, there's no work at all. In the winter of 1963, there was no work for six weeks straight. On Christmas Eve, when a nearby schoolteacher brought a package of donated clothing, there were no Christmas presents in the Newton house. And there was no food.

There are tens of thousands of Darell Graveses and Ray Newtons in Appalachia, exiled from the rest of society and its prosperity, deserted by their jobs and by their union, a society on the dole.

Today they are famous: the magazines and television documentaries have made them so. Their fame is new, but their plight is not. For nearly a decade, they near-starved in obscurity. And the best anyone could think to do about it was the dole: relief; wel-

No need to resort to leaf-raking . . . there are fouled streams to be cleaned; auto graveyards and trash heaps to be removed.

fare; a monthly handout of some starchy surplus food. Even in this work-worshipping culture, nobody could bring themselves to provide work—massive numbers of here-and-now jobs for the massive number of able-bodied idle of Appalachia. Everyone behaved as if paralyzed—paralyzed, perhaps, by a fear of returning to boondoggling, to "leaf-raking."

Not that there was any need to resort to leaf-raking or boondoggling. Not that there wasn't plenty to be done. There are naked hillsides to be reforested; slopes, ravaged and gutted by the ruin-and-run strip miners, to be reclaimed and restored to nature. There are fouled streams to be cleaned, and auto graveyards and trash heaps by stream and road to be removed, and dams to be built to end the threat of flood and to form lakes to bring tourists to this land of exile.

Not that all this couldn't be afforded. The richest country in the world can afford to do anything it sets its mind to. Even fly to the moon.

Yet Appalachia remains a society on the dole—the prospective beneficiary, to be sure, of some "long-range" solutions that hopefully will mean some more jobs five, ten or twenty years from now. But what about the present? What about the men rotting in idleness now?

And what of their children? What of young James Monroe Newton, living by that railroad track in Eastern Kentucky? This is a boy with a brightness in his eye and a spark in his soul. You approach the Newton cabin and he looks up fleetingly from the serious business of fixing his coal-hauling wagon. He needs that wagon, for in winter he is up before daybreak and over with coal and wagon to the schoolhouse where, for fifty cents a week each, he starts the potbellied stoves that heat the three classrooms. His earnings he spends buying "baccy" for his mother, candy for himself and his brothers and sisters, and contributing to the March of Dimes.

Must young James Monroe Newton be sentenced to live another five or ten years in a society on the dole? Must he grow up led to believe, by the daily evidence before his eyes, that for most men there is not, and apparently cannot be, the opportunity simply to provide for their families? Is this the best the richest nation in the world can do for him and those around him?

24

Must young J... five or ten years

the exiles

through affluent eyes

PORTRAIT OF A COUNTY: * Population (1960
census): 30,102. Median income (1960): $2,615
(national average: $5,660). Percentage of people
receiving surplus food: 25% (national average: 3%).
Percentage of people receiving welfare: 9% (national average: 4%). Unemployment (1963): 10.6%
(national average: 5.7%.)

* Letcher County, Kentucky.

26   38

"There's no unemployment problem in this county."

"THERE's no unemployment problem in this county," a successful lawyer tells you. "After all, a man's not really unemployed unless he wants to work and can't find a job. The truth is, the men around here don't *want* to work. They'd rather have handouts."

He points through his office window to where the ground has been cleared for a new courthouse. "How many men do you suppose applied for jobs on that building? Just guess. Five hundred? Why, we had to scratch to get a hundred and fifty. See what I mean? People around here don't want jobs."

You go down to the courthouse building project and ask some questions. How many jobs are there for untrained local labor? Maybe a dozen. Did they advertise the jobs in the local paper? No. On the radio? No. You go over to the food line a block away. In the line, the wife of an ex-carpenter. Had she or her husband heard of the jobs on the courthouse project? No. They take no newspaper; they own no radio. The only time they get to town is to pick up their surplus food allotment.

Talk to the most successful strip mine operator in town. He's angry about the spate of magazine articles depicting the poverty of his community. He shows you the figures on bank deposits: up over last year. (But *whose* deposits?) Stick around 'til Saturday, he urges, to see Main Street jammed with shoppers. (But how many people are stranded and hidden away up in the creeks and hollows who haven't seen Main Street for months?)

Back to the lawyer. How would he feel about a massive public works program to put all these loafers to work? "That would be fine—so long as they really *work*. I wouldn't want any shovel-leaning. People ought to *work* for what the government gives them." (Later you learn that the lawyer is drawing $1,500 a year from the government as compensation for a wartime injury—justified on the premise that it has impaired his earning capacity. But the injury has been so successfully treated, at government expense, that it does not appear to inhibit in any way his career as a lawyer—a profession he was able to enter thanks to the GI Bill of Rights).

It would be wrong, of course, to picture Appalachia—or any other society—as peopled entirely by men eager to grasp every morsel of work. But if you have only a fourth-grade education and you haven't worked for months—or years—and you've established a steady $125 a month on welfare, it's a dubious bargain to give up even that meager amount for a job you know—or fear—is here today and gone next month or next week. Besides, the will to work, like any muscle, will atrophy if allowed to fall into disuse. There are some men of forty in Appalachia who have never had a job.

The irony and tragedy of Appalachia, observes one life-long citizen, is that "we allowed our wealth—our coal—to be pulled out of the earth and shipped away, without a penny of tax. We never educated our people or built them decent schools. We abused our people. But when technology came, we replaced *them* first."

28

"Farmin' ain't much when you can work the whole year long and come Christmas, you can't even buy your child an apple."

farmer

JOHN PATTERSON, farm-born and farm-bred, devotes most of his daylight hours to trying to support his wife and four children and raise a decent stand of cotton on too few acres of too sandy soil in Northern Arkansas.

Patterson's house speaks of his want: front porch broken and drooping; plastic sheeting over the windows concealing the absence of glass; no running water—every drop has to be hauled from a spring two miles away. The government has appraised the house. Its value: $600.

Nearby, the emptiness of a once-full barn is silhouetted against the trees.

John is too poor to own a tractor. He still "plows a mule." When the plow blade strikes a rock, the handle hits him in the stomach and fairly knocks the wind out of him. ("I've walked along this land many a time trying to get my breath back.")

29

"Kids don't want to be scratchin' around a farm. There ain't no livin' in it now."

The work is hard and the rewards meager: $150 last year for selling livestock; $235 for his cotton and hay. The only thing that separates him and his family from starvation is a $696 disability pension from World War II.

He owes $960—more than half of it for doctors' and hospital bills for his arthritic wife. He owes the local bank $400. Interest rate: 10 per cent.

Next year's budget is carefully planned. To clothe a family of six: less than four dollars a week. For their "health" needs: two dollars a week. For "household operating expenses," five dollars a month. For "house repairs," forty dollars for the year.

Like all cotton farmers, John Patterson gets a government subsidy. Eight and a half cents a pound. But you can't grow much cotton on a few acres of poor soil—not, at any rate, without a lot of fertilizer, and John Patterson can't afford much of that. His total subsidy last year: $75.

Eight and a half cents, the subsidy is, on as many pounds of cotton as a person can grow and sell. In a nearby county is a 4,000-acre cotton farm. It is not owned by a farmer like John Patterson. It is owned by a corporation: St. Francis Valley Farms (a division

"We ain't nothin' but a grasshopper in the sight of God. You can plant cotton and fertilize it and chop it, but if you don't get the water from above, you ain't done nothin'."

of E. Ritter and Company). *Its* subsidy: $301,700—more than four thousand times John Patterson's.

John Patterson lives on his farm and works it himself. He is no absentee owner. The same cannot be said of all cotton farms. Near Phoenix, Arizona, for example, a 4,400-acre cotton farm is jointly owned by the Arizona Title Insurance and Trust Company and the Del E. Webb Development Company. Owned by a company, operated by a company: J. G. Boswell Company. Subsidy: $560,745. Nearly eight thousand Patterson-size subsidies.

There are about 650,000 small cotton farmers like John Patterson. They constitute more than seventy per cent of all cotton farmers. They get just seven per cent of the total cotton subsidy.

Their average subsidy is $63 a year. The average subsidy for the three hundred and twenty-two largest cotton farmers in America: $113,000.

In fact, just seventy-eight large farmers in California and Arizona alone receive more in cotton subsidies than all the 275,000 John Pattersons in five Southeastern states.

John Patterson's subsidy is low because his farm is small and he produces little. If he had some machinery—a "bush whacker" and a tractor—he could clear and work more land, grow more and make more. If he could buy fertilizer, he could coax a better crop out of the ground—he wouldn't have to thin out his cotton every year to keep from starving it.

But machinery and fertilizer take money. Where is John Patterson to get it? The local bank won't lend him any more. And the Federal government is too poor, it seems, to give him a loan.

Too poor? The Federal government—with a hundred billion dollar budget—too *poor?*

Well, put it this way: the government can afford three billion dollars for cotton and other price-support subsidies—most of which completely bypass the likes of John Patterson. But for loans to

*"I'm out in the deep part now. I either got to sink or swim. But I ain't gonna
sell my farm. I think I'll fight it a while yet."*

small farmers such as he, it can afford less than a tenth of that. There just isn't enough to reach John Patterson.

(The government can afford three billion dollars for price-support subsidies, but only one twenty-fifth as much for loans to help the John Pattersons fix up their tumble-down houses. For housing *grants* to farmers too poor to repay a loan, not a penny.)

Now while a government loan—or maybe a combination loan and grant—could make a big difference to John Patterson, while it could pull him away from the edge of insolvency, it would not be the whole answer. It would not, for example, answer the question of his children's future. One of the four could stay and inherit this one-family farm. But what about the other three?

The root problem of the Ozarks and other impoverished rural areas is that with the growing use of machinery, technology, and fertilizers, fewer men can bring greater yields from the earth. Men and jobs are being pushed off the farms. One person in three in the Ozarks is on relief. The need is for off-farm jobs. The need is to bring industry and employment to the country.

The government has a program designed to do just that. It's called Rural Renewal, supposedly the farmers' version of Urban Renewal. Out of a six billion dollar Agriculture Department budget, Rural Renewal in 1964 got $1,200,000—about one six-thousandth of the total. (Congress was asked to provide over two million dollars; it cut the request in half.)

John Patterson is lucky. He owns his farm. But more than half of the farmers like him don't. They work somebody else's land. Most of them would fare far better if they could own their own farms (those who have bought land through government loans have managed to triple their income by the time they finish repaying the loan). But often they find themselves stymied by inflated land values. The reason: more and more, farmers find themselves bidding for land not against other farmers, but against doctors and lawyers and executives in distant cities, many of them taking advantage of a tax "angle," and hence willing to pay considerably more than the pure farming value of the land.

There's a way of attacking that problem, too: have nonprofit

"A guy's got to be pretty nervy to stick with farmin'."

or government corporations buy farm land when it comes on the market and sell it to farmers at its "unwatered" or true farm value. But some in Congress labeled this plan "Communistic," and stopped it dead in its tracks.

Some say John Patterson has no business being in farming. He is too small, too "inefficient," they say. But are we to pass judgment that *only* the large corporate farms deserve to survive? And since when is efficiency the *only* yardstick in the American economy? (If it is, then we should lose no time repealing all government subsidies and tariffs, so that only the most naturally "efficient" will survive.)

John Patterson isn't a mere machine, to be calibrated and judged by his pure efficiency. He is a human being, born and brought up on his farm. And he is there, with his family, doing the only thing he knows how to do. His life is hard. He knows he'll never make much money at farming. He is convinced he will end up like his aged parents living nearby: on welfare. But he wouldn't leave his farm for anything.

"You take to where a man has been on a farm all his life. You can move him out of the country, but you won't take the country life out of him.

"I'd ruther be on a farm as anywhere . . . if I could just stay even with the world."

portfolio:

poverty

in the southwest

Bea is now fifteen. Her baby is fifteen months old.

a mendelian tale

of four sisters

IN the core of Chicago are four sisters, the living embodiment of an iron law of heredity that Mendel never taught: that the poverty and ignorance of the parent can be visited on the child and the child's child just as inexorably as brown eyes or blue, dark hair or blond, white skin or black.

Two of the four sisters live in the same slum house. Upstairs: Essie. Eight children. No husband. Downstairs: Florence. Five children. No husband. A block away: Cecile. Five children. No husband. Two blocks away: Beatrice. Six children. No husband.

All told, twenty-four children, but no husband-father to bring them up. Not surprising. The four are only living as their mother lived and as they lived as children in Memphis, Tennessee. Like mother, like daughter.

Florence has a daughter, Hazel. Hazel is seventeen. Her baby is already nearly two. Upstairs, Essie's daughter, Gladys, is now fifteen. *Her* baby is fifteen months old. Like mother, like daughter, like granddaughter.

In Memphis, the mother of these four sisters got as far as the second grade. The sisters did better: one of them got to the fifth. Essie's daughter, Edna, has gone further than her mother. At age seventeen she got to the seventh grade. Then she quit. Ask her

how much is three times three. After a struggle, she gets it right—
on the second try. Edna's last school was a correction school for
errant girls.

Essie has a son, Robert. He is nearing the end of the third
grade. Ask him to show you his homework. He takes out his reader
and opens it. Below the pictures of fair-skinned, pink-cheeked children are these words, with which third-grade Robert struggles:

Let's see the mother and the father.
See the baby.
Where is the baby?
The mother cannot see.
The father cannot see.

Where can Robert do his homework? There is no light in the "living room," nor any table. The kitchen is a little better: there is a 40-watt naked bulb overhead, and a table of sorts. Also the only sink in the place. Also, behind the door, the only toilet. Which makes this the most heavily-trafficked of the three rooms—which Robert shares with eight others.

And who helps him with his homework? Not sister Edna— she's little better off than he. Not his mother. She barely finished the fourth grade. Besides, she's got seven other kids and one grandchild to look after.

Downstairs, Florence has a son, Charles. He is sixteen. He is just out of school: reform school. He is out of school and out of work. He doesn't want to go back to school; he says he wants to work. But what jobs are there for an uneducated boy of sixteen? And where does he start looking?

He doesn't. He hangs around all day. *Next* week he'll start looking.

Next week he'll start looking for work.

the unwanted

LUCILLE CAMPBELL has six children. She is twenty-seven. Her oldest child is fourteen.

Lucille Campbell has never been married. Each of the children was unplanned and unwanted. But no one ever told her how to prevent having children—not until she had had five. Then she was given a diaphragm. That worked fine—until she was raped one dark night on her way home. Now she has six children.

The seven of them, plus Lucille's mother, crowd into three rat-infested rooms in a Chicago slum.

No one should be surprised that Lucille Campbell had never been taught about birth control. Welfare workers in Chicago are forbidden to broach the subject to their "clients." The state of Illinois gives some help in birth control—to married women living with their husbands. Where the children-to-be must grow up with no father, help is denied.

Consider this: as recently as two years ago, the birth rate among Negroes in Cook County, Illinois (Chicago), was as high as it is in India.

Consider this: each unwanted child costs the taxpayers of Cook County $13,000—merely to support and educate to age seventeen. The cost of providing birth control help to a relief mother: $30 a year.

Basement living—the last hope of keeping a family off the street.

"If you don't have a husband, it's not a good idea to have children, but after you have them, what you gonna do?"

Consider this: Cook County spends 8.5 million dollars a month —more than $100 million a year—in support of dependent children, many if not most of whom were unplanned and unwanted.

Then consider this: Cook County does not spend one penny providing birth control help to its citizens.

There are, for many, moral objections to birth control. Those must be weighed.

You go to visit the Ross family, and you see the life to which the ten Ross children have been sentenced. Not that these children asked to be born. Not that Mrs. Ross wanted ten children. But they are here.

"*I didn't want to get started having babies, but after I got started, there wasn't
nothin' I could do about it.*"

On the door of the Ross house, a sign: CONDEMNED. Unfit for human habitation. The sign has been there for four months. For four months the Rosses have been trying to find a place that would take ten children. No luck. It's not so much that Mr. Ross doesn't have the money. He has a construction job. He could pay $100 a month rent, he says. The problem is the kids. There just are no houses for $100 that will take ten children—or six or seven, for that matter.

Time has run out. The marshals are due in a few hours to come and nail up the door that shouts CONDEMNED. In a few hours, the Rosses, their children and their belongings (such as they are) will be on the street.

You go with Mr. Ross to look at his last hope of keeping his family off the street. It's not a house. It's not even an apartment. It's a basement furnace room. No toilet or washbasin (the Rosses will have bathroom "privileges" upstairs); no stove (cooking for twelve people will have to be done on an electric hot plate); bare concrete floor (on which the Rosses will throw mattresses—they'll never get a bed down those narrow stairs); only one tiny window, behind the furnace, flush with the sidewalk outdoors. Twelve people will spend two-thirds of every twenty-four hours jammed together in this basement furnace room.

Mr. Ross looks at it. "What can you do when your hands are tied? And mine are tied with a ball and knot."

So this is where the Ross children will live out the next part of their sentence. This is where they'll spend Christmas. Not that they asked to live this way. Not that Mrs. Ross wanted them to live this way. But they are there.

You consider the moral objections to birth control.

And you wonder.

59

life sentence

It is hard for the affluent to comprehend, the despair of the poor. It has become a cliché, and, as with all clichés, been drained of meaning.

Perhaps the clearest perception of it came not from the resident of a slum or a ghetto, but from a man now living in a modest yet adequate house in the country, a man who, in his struggling days, lived for a year in New York's "Little Italy." It was a grim, brutal year. But, he now recalls, "I had an escape hatch. My wife's uncle had some money. We weren't imprisoned there.

"But if I had thought that that one year was a mandatory life sentence, I would have shriveled up and died."

In what calls itself a "hotel," in the heart of Chicago's cruel Maxwell Street slums, first floor right, Roberta Clark is living out such a life sentence in a single room furnished with a bed, a single stick chair and two dressers. The cooking facilities consist of a single-burner hot plate set on an orange crate. ("Really I don't cook," says Roberta Clark. "I just muck up the food to keep from starving.") There is a tiny basin in the corner of the room, but no hot water (except what she heats herself) and no toilet. The toilet she uses is out in the hall—a blackened fixture in an unlit room, shared by all the women on the first floor of the "hotel." But, she says, "I don't go out in the hall at night. It's dangerous. After that sun goes down I don't open my door. What goes on out there I don't know. I just don't open that door." At night, the toilet is beyond her reach.

How old is she? "My mother didn't know how to read and write, so I don't know how old I am. I'm either sixty-seven or sixty-nine."

So Roberta Clark is nearer than some to the end of her life imprisonment. But she wants out.

"*Please* get me a home. If you get me out of this building, you'll do a wonder to my heart and mind."

"Please get me a home. If you get me out of this building, you'll do a wonder to my heart and mind."

portfolio:

poverty's elders

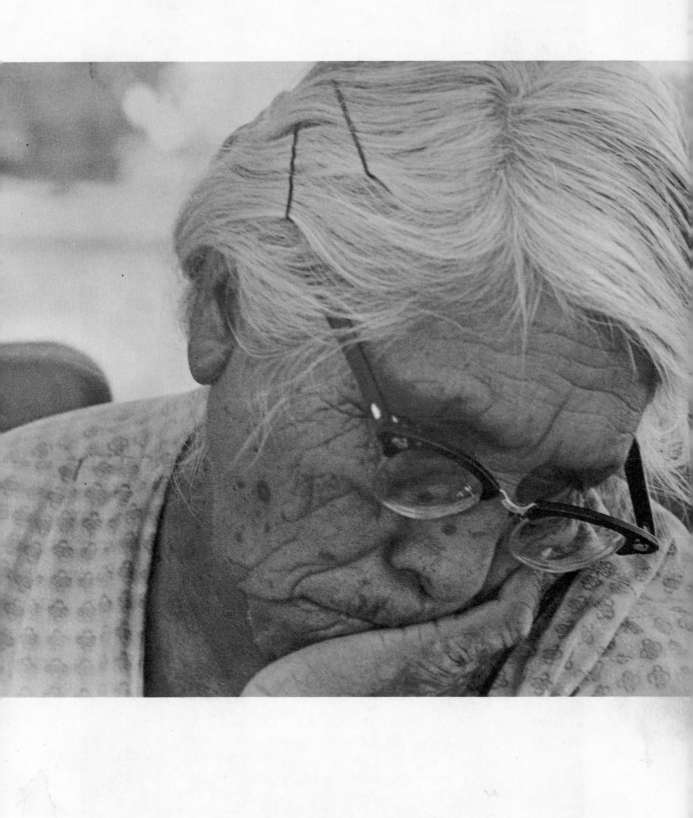

the samaritan as cop

THREE A.M. A knock on the door. In some countries, a probable political arrest. In an American city slum, an equally fearful threat: a member of the "special investigation unit" of the welfare department paying a surprise nocturnal visit, invading the home of an unwed welfare mother in search of a man in the house—grounds, under the regulations, for cutting her off the welfare rolls.

The teen-age son answers the door. Two men push past him. They don't identify themselves. They go to where the mother and younger daughter are sleeping in a single bed. They find no man in the house. They depart without apology. Weeks later, the incident is repeated—this time at one in the morning. Same result: no man in the house.

In another household, the surprise visit comes earlier in the evening. The mother is taking a bath. The special investigator pushes aside a nine-year-old daughter, searches the bedroom, all closets, invades the privacy of the bathroom. He finds no man, but emerges triumphant: there is a man's suit in the closet. The mother tells him it belonged to her dead husband. She fails to convince the investigator. She is cut off the welfare rolls.

A new and unplanned child is born to a slum mother. Who is the father? She has no way of knowing. There are several possibilities: like many a lonely, frightened and deserted woman, she has been a pushover for any man who so much as hints at security— or maybe just some occasional affectionate companionship. But society self-righteously insists on knowing who the father is. No father, no welfare help for the new child.

But the child must be provided for. Her moral duty is plain: pick up some "wino" on the street. Not too proud a man—a man who can be induced by five dollars (if she has it) or a roll in the hay (if she doesn't) to go into the welfare office and claim to be the father of the child.

This done, society's conscience is satisfied.

Rosalie Johnson has six children. Her husband is sent to Federal narcotics prison. She moves in with her sister, Helen Rankin, also the mother of six. A costly move for Helen Rankin: she is cut off the welfare rolls. Why? Because presumably her sister can now take care of her children during the day. Ipso facto. Helen Rankin is now, under the welfare regulations, "employable." The regulations are indifferent to whether there are any jobs available to a woman of her meager training and experience. Her kids are now taken care of (whether properly or not is also beside the point), and she is now officially classified as "employable." Which is to say, ineligible for further welfare.

For a while, the two mothers and their twelve children manage to survive on Rosalie's welfare check. But soon, this too ends abruptly: she violates the moral code which society lays down for its wards: she has an illegitimate child. She is told she must look to the child's father for support.

Society renders a judgment against the mother, and metes out a sentence against the children: they are relegated to the hopelessly overcrowded "shelter" the city provides for such children. There, their immediate support will cost society many times the welfare payments that have now been denied their mother. There they may stay for years, being molded efficaciously (though unintentionally) into permanent dependents of society, so socially crippled that they may one day end up dispatching their own children to this institution (many alumni have).

Thus society punishes the children. And in the process, it punishes itself.

> "To the degree feasible, it is . . .
> the purpose of public assistance . . .
> to maintain and strengthen family life."
> —*Statement of Philosophy and*
> *Practice of the Public Assist-*
> *ance Division, (Washington)*
> *D. C. Department of Public Welfare.*

James Henry finds it hard to believe that anyone would bribe him to desert his family. But to him, there is no other way of looking at his situation.

James Henry is out of work: the filling station where he had been making $100 a week has fallen victim to a new highway project. He has tried to find another job, but he is too old. And he is a Negro. He is unable to support his wife and seven children, but as long as he remains with them, the city will not support them either. Under the regulations, there can be no assistance to families where there is an "employable" father in the house.

It is plain to him what society wants him to do, and he dutifully does it: he deserts his family, goes off to another state, his wife believes, to find a job. She hopes he will send for her. In the meantime, says a report on the James Henry family, "his three-year-old daughter cries herself to sleep each night, clutching her father's picture."

High on society's list of apprehensions, it seems, is a fear that its wards might get rich on the dole.

A welfare family, pressed for payment of its bills, takes out a loan of $177.75. The Welfare Department finds out about it. The loan is considered "outside income." The welfare check is reduced accordingly. The creditors' pressure persists. The father forges a check. He is now in prison.

A welfare worker discovers that sixteen years previously, the now-deceased husband of his client received an inheritance that was not reported to the welfare authorities. Her monthly check is all of $91.39; but from this, the caseworker decides, $8.71—nearly ten per cent of her worldly income—must be deducted each month, until the full amount of the inheritance has been "repaid." That will take fourteen years.

A salty, but clearly senile, eighty-three-year-old tells his welfare worker how he has earned $400 by going to sea again. Without even checking the story, the worker effects monthly deductions from the welfare check until the full $400 fantasy has been repaid.

An elderly welfare "client," anxious to make advance arrangements for what she feels is her impending death, cashes in her life insurance policy for $200, receives $168 from her daughter, and purchases a prepaid funeral for $368. The daughter's gift, says the welfare department, constitutes a "new resource." Her monthly grant is suspended for two months, and is only reinstated on condition that the $168 be repaid, by monthly deductions from her welfare check.

"Unable to determine your need . . ."

You stand in the "living room" of Doris Hunt's grimy three-room house. You look at the furniture, the grease-laden walls, the broken plaster, the faulty heater. Staring up at you is a half-clad boy of eight or nine, his absurdly oversized trousers held up precariously by a piece of rope. You can't believe the piece of paper Doris has handed you—Assistance Form PW-PA-16. It announces that Doris's welfare check is being "held." The caseworker's handwriting offers an "explanation:"

> "We are unable to determine your need because it is our understanding that you own a car."

You are in Doris's house because the school principal has told you her children are notoriously late for school. And for a reason: many mornings, Doris has no breakfast to give them. To spare herself the pain and shame of admitting this fact to them, she deliberately lets them sleep too late and then hustles them off to school with the claim there's "no time" for breakfast. A common practice in Doris's neighborhood. The school principal says many children vomit from malnutrition.

Yet under welfare rules and regulations, the unconfirmed rumor that Doris Hunt owns a car—never mind whether it's a $100 jalopy or a $7,000 Cadillac—renders the caseworker and welfare officialdom "unable to determine her need." (Television sets, no matter how ancient, or how wispy the picture, can be another sign of impermissible affluence.)

And so the welfare check that means food and shelter for Doris and her children is being held up for God knows how long not because it is a verified fact, but because "it is our understanding" that she owns a car.

A five-minute phone call to the registry of motor vehicles establishes the truth: Doris Hunt owns no car. That phone call is made by the school principal to whom Doris takes her case. Not by the caseworker. (It takes the caseworker how long—five minutes perhaps?—to fill out Assistance Form PW-PA-16.)

Doris Hunt's house breathes "need," but more than mere financial need. Need for education not of the classroom variety (although Doris has had little enough of that) but education in the rudiments of living: simple things such as feeding her children at regular times, instead of giving her nine-year-old a quarter at 8:30 at night and telling him to run off and get a cupcake and a coke. Simple things, such as how to get the grease off the walls and put some pride in that house; how to plan and buy sensible food and clothing for her children; or how to budget her month's welfare check. With some patient help and guidance from her caseworker, Doris could probably feed her kids a regular breakfast—all month. But she needs the help; she needs the guidance—and a full measure of patience.

But the caseworker has other preoccupations. She has other "clients"—a hundred and thirty-eight others. Far too many. Hard to give much guidance to a hundred and thirty-nine families, even if she spent full-time on home visits. But those are only a small part of the job. There's the paper work: forms to fill out (a hundred and seventy-five varieties), reports to write, records to keep. Out of a five-day week, at least three—more often four—are spent not with

families but behind an office desk. Only one or two days a week—maybe eight or nine days a month—"in the field."

And, of course, there are the regulations—the job of keeping tabs on the "clients" to make sure the regulations are observed. Is it true that Mrs. A owns a car? What about that TV set in Mrs. B's house? Did she use welfare money to buy it? What of the rumor that Mrs. C has a boy friend? Shouldn't *he* be supporting her and the children? Couldn't Mrs. D's grandmother take care of the D children so that Mrs. D would be "employable?" Is Mrs. E earning more on that part-time job than the regulations allow?

A caseworker has many preoccupations.

What sort of society are we?

Two of our citizens—a welfare mother and her landlord—violate the rules laid down for them.

The welfare mother's transgressions: suspicion of owning a car; having a man's suit in the closet; inability to produce the father of her illegitimate child. The sentence against her: withhold the means of her livelihood.

Her landlord's transgressions: exposed electrical wiring; ancient and inaccessible fire extinguishers; rats and rat holes; leaky plumbing; standing water. The sentence against him is probably long delayed (the landlord has his pals in the building inspector's office and a lawyer wise in the ways of legal stalling tactics); when it comes, it is a mere tap on the wrist—a five-dollar-per-violation fine, far less painful than the cost of repairing the wiring and the plumbing and getting rid of the rats.

Two of our citizens receive government handouts: a fatherless welfare family and a California cotton farmer.

The welfare family's handout? Depends on where the family lives. In Alabama, the average handout for the fatherless family (three children): less than eleven dollars a week. In New York, where these handouts are the highest: about forty-five dollars a week. To receive this bounty, the family must toe the mark: one misstep and off the dole. And the family must live lean: no cars, no TVs, no outside income. No one must luxuriate or get rich on the government handout.

The cotton farmer's handout comes to a million and a half dollars a year—thirty thousand dollars a week. No one bats an eye. The sky's the limit. The more cotton he can grow, the bigger the handout.

We are very moral about our wards. Fornication, for example, may be punishable by starvation. But that's not all. We also shame our wards into producing false fathers for their illegitimate children. We bribe them to desert their families. We are very moral about our wards.

They need our help; they need to be taught. But all too often we don't help or teach. We are too busy being cops.

a plea for

an end to tongue clucking

QUESTION: If a child at a party were to eat with his fingers instead of with spoon or fork, whom would you blame—the parents? Or the untaught child?

WALK into a south side Chicago slum apartment house. On the ground floor, an apartment in chaos: clothes strewn over floors and furniture or stuffed into the handiest corner; half-emptied plates or cups left wherever they were put down; open packages and boxes and jars of food amid uncleaned pans on a littered kitchen table; on the beds, unwashed gray-brown sheets—or, perhaps, stained, bare mattresses; toilet stained an ugly dark color, its top missing; broken plaster, broken mirror, broken light fixtures.

A human pigsty—shown you by one of its shamefaced occupants, an unshaven, unwashed and malodorous middle-aged man.

Shameful? Look more closely. There are no closets, no kitchen cabinets, no place to store anything. No kitchen sink (that went when what used to be one apartment was cut up to make three)—only a tiny basin, too small to wash clothes. Look into the shower stall: it's stacked half full with dirty clothes; the shower hasn't worked in a year. Hot water? None; the hot water heater hasn't worked for three months (the landlord is going to fix it any day now). Ask more questions. How many living here? Nine, in three rooms, with two beds and a battered sofa to share among them. Where did the family come from? Mississippi. Former abode: a dirt-floored shack. Education: none.

Meet the apartment manager. Listen to his tale of unexplained leaks into a ground-floor apartment—unexplained until he went into the apartment above to find a family from deep in the Southern mountain country throwing buckets of water on the floor and sweeping it with a broom. What other way *is* there to clean a dirty floor?

Go up one more flight. Visit the immaculate apartment of a neatly dressed but husbandless young mother. Formal education: little more than the Mississippi family living in squalor two floors below. Informal education: a different matter—a childhood with a grandmother endowed with a strong will, a sharp tongue, and a taste for neatness and cleanliness.

Simply a matter of teaching. *And* of surroundings. Look out the window of any slum apartment or house. Or of a slum school where children supposedly do their learning. Trash. Litter. Empty bottles. Garbage. Clean up a slum house—and what have you escaped from?

You're driving through a slum. You finish a package of cigarettes. You crumple up the used pack and roll down the car window. You check yourself: long-taught habit tells you to put it in the car ashtray. You look around—and you throw the pack into a trash-strewn empty lot. Why not? What have you added—a tenth—a hundredth of one per cent to the filth that's already there?

Among the morally righteous in most communities, an unmarried girl with four children, or five or eight, provokes a clucking of tongues

Clean up a slum house, and what have you escaped from?

and a raising of eyebrows. But who ever taught this girl the means of preventing unwanted childbirth? In the community in which she and the tongue-cluckers live, how much is the local government spending on *that* sort of education?

But (say the tongue-cluckers) it is not so much a matter of education as it is a matter of morals. Yet is it all so simple? What, for instance, is the moral duty of a mother of four, faced with eviction, with no apparent way of preventing her children and her belongings from being thrown out on the street, and approached by a friendly man with a truck to move the belongings—and a normal male appetite? "If a man has anything and offers to help you out," says one prisoner of the slums, "you don't say to him, 'But you'll have to marry me first.' You take what he offers right off and offer what you have in return. Of course you hope that some day he'll want to make it legal. But beggars can't be choosers."

A Negro woman—the mother of six, by six different fathers—expressed it in a letter:

> As far back as I can remember I were taught sex were something bad But yet as I grew up among the poor class of my race I could see an hear of women having (sex) relation for survival what I mean as far back as my grandmother mother and also out of my family women had to have sex relation with men for shose, clothing, more food with most of us not just for kicks. We come from bad backgrounds. Most of us now days were born into this world in this fashion our parents weren't really married father or mother had lover's on the side we weren't taught respect and about sex our father or mother were low rated in our presents we saw our parents having sexual relation with her lovers. But we have no real future not the poor class— if I could I would get able and get out of this for I know my children hasn't and won't ever see me doing such, but yes I have failed in just giving life to them.

three youths of the ghetto

"I GOT a lot of ideas, but I got a brick wall standing in my way, and soon my ideas is going to fade."

John Ash is talking. A moody boy of seventeen with ambition in his heart and poetry on his tongue.

John is a dropout, but he doesn't fit the stereotype. Let him show you the books he's been reading: Barbara Ward, James Baldwin, Charles Dickens (fished out of a garbage pail), a book on semantics.

John is a dropout by necessity, not by choice. His girl is pregnant. ("My father tried to teach me about sex and how to protect myself, but I didn't listen, and now I got a family coming.") For him, school is finished. For him, it's go to work (*if* he can get a job) and get married.

The place John calls home is an unlikely place to find Dickens, Barbara Ward and a book on semantics. You get to it by walking down six worn wooden steps from the ghetto street, through a steel fire door, and into a basement corridor: narrow, dingy, brick-lined, bare-bulb lit. The corridor soon widens into the room where the "super" keeps the trash cans and other building paraphernalia. (John's family also uses the room—illegally—as a spill-over from their cramped four rooms: there's a bureau and some chairs, and a dirty rug on the floor.)

By the side of the corridor, you find the undersized Ash apartment, and the ghost of John's near-past: his younger brothers and sisters. In the television commercial which monopolizes their attention, a white child tempts them with toys they will never enjoy. ("You'll *love* getting outfits for Barbie and Ken to go with the ones for Alan and Midge.")

For John's brother, Calvin, age eleven, reading is a torturously slow affair, in which punctuation is unnoticed, the word "gentle" unfamiliar, and the word "photograph," when sounded for him, a surprise ("It doesn't have any f's in it!" he exclaims). Nathaniel's only playground is the street. ("Yeah, there's a park around here, but my friends say there's a red lady there and if she scratches you on the neck, you'll die. So I don't go to the park.")

Calvin's older brother, John, has an ambition: to start a youth labor union, so that kids in the ghetto will have some bargaining power when they go to work. But no one's going to pay John for starting a union of kids. And he's got to get paid. He's *got* to get a job. He's got a family on the way. ("I need a job, but I ain't got the schooling.")

You sense John will keep on plugging away. But he doesn't know what to do about that brick wall in front of him.

He's afraid all his ideas, all his ambitions, are going to fade. But he'll keep plugging.

"You try to move a little faster," he says, "so the world won't leave you behind with your head in your hands."

The most striking thing about Little Joe is his eyes. You take a close, hard look at them. Those are not the eyes of a thirteen-year old. In other respects—in size, in movement—Little Joe is thirteen. But those eyes—hard, cunning—belong to a person of, what? —twenty-one? Thirty?

Little Joe is precocious—after a fashion. At thirteen, he is already an alumnus of Youth House, the detention home for young delinquents. He was put there, his mother says, for snatching money from a taxi driver—he and another boy.

And so at thirteen, Little Joe has a record. It will stick to him like his shadow the rest of his life. ("Ever been arrested, son?" "Yes, sir." "Well, we'll call you if we have any openings.") The ghetto is full of men and boys with records who willingly share their tales of futility and self-pity with the likes of Little Joe. And so, as far as he can see, Little Joe is all washed up. At thirteen.

Has he learned a lesson from his month in Youth House? "Not too good," his mother says. Afternoons, you are likely to find those hard eyes of Little Joe's looking for a game of blackjack, roaming the streets with a pack of boys mostly older than he is, a deck of cards and a couple of dollar bills in his pocket.

Visit Little Joe's home and you'll get some clues to his juvenile precociousness. Walk up the five flights, the eighty-five steps; approach the metal door to Little Joe's apartment. Just outside that door, another flight of steps leading to the roof, and bearing the

"All they do around here is sit on the stoop all day and talk about which girl's going to have a baby next."

tell-tale signs of a "shooting gallery" where junkies "take off": translucent paper envelopes that once contained heroin; burnt matches and a bottle cap (the "cooker"); a king-sized Coke bottle filled with clear water to be drawn up into the crude eyedropper syringe; a jar of bloodstained water used by one "cat" to clean out "the works" (eyedropper and needle) before passing them on to the next "cat."

This is what Little Joe has grown up with, he and his eight brothers and sisters. And it's what the unborn brother or sister in his mother's belly will grow up with, too, because no one is going to do anything about this "shooting gallery" right outside Little Joe's door. (If a visitor can find the remains of that gallery, so could the police. But they don't.)

As is the case with one out of every three children in the ghetto, there is no father in Little Joe's home. You ask his mother what she

In the ghetto, one man out of every four has no job.

tells her kids about what goes on outside that door. "You don't have to tell them nothing," she says. "They know. Even the little ones say, 'the junkies are out there again.'"

She'd like to get her kids out of there. For five years she's been applying to get into public housing—"the project," she calls it. "But they just write you and tell you you're still 'on file.'"

At the school Little Joe attends sporadically, teachers keep a sharp lookout for sex play. In school, the bathrooms are watched. At home, it's four boys to a bed (Little Joe and three brothers), every night of their lives. In the next room, two sisters share a bed with their brother.

What's the future for these children? Little Joe's mother raises her eyebrows questioningly, "I don't know, really. That's what I wonder myself, sometimes."

Cora is sixteen. Cora is pregnant. Her boy friend says he would like to marry her. But he doesn't have a job. So it looks as though the baby is going to be a bastard.

It is not altogether surprising that Cora is pregnant. Not that she's a lascivious girl. Actually, she is shy, quiet, anything but flirtatious. But young pregnancies are the norm in the tenements. There are five girls in her building who are pregnant. One of them is thirteen. Another fourteen. The boy wanted to marry the fourteen-year-old. But he couldn't. She is under age.

What about the neighborhood that Cora's grown up in? "Not long ago a man came up to me on the street and said he could teach me how to be a drug addict and a prostitute at the same time, and live fine, right here on this block. He told me if I'd get my friends, he'd teach them, too."

And in the next block, she says, are "junkies, taking their stuff and bothering girls—and even sleeping on the streets."

Cora's friend, Dolly, is the neighborhood commentator. "If these girls are going to do it anyway," she says, "their mothers should tell them how to have sex relations and not have babies. I think they should put out more books about it. Some mothers don't know how to express themselves to their kids."

Cora doesn't want to bring up her baby in the ghetto. "All they do around here is sit on the stoop all day and talk about who's going to have a baby next. A woman who's mad at my mother keeps bugging her about my being pregnant; she doesn't even know her own daughter's pregnant. I don't want to bring up my kid around stuff like that."

Cora would like to be a stenographer. But how? She doesn't have the training. And even if she did get a job, who would care for her child?

Is she scared to be having a baby, alone, at sixteen? "Yeah, a little. But I'll get over it."

These three youths of the ghetto have one thing in common: all have made a misstep, early in life—a misstep that will probably scar their lives forever.

John has knocked up a girl. He's forced out of school and into a job market for which he will be permanently ill-prepared.

Cora is pregnant. She, too, will be a school dropout. With above-average luck, she'll marry. But with just average luck, she'll never have a legal marriage. Instead, she'll spend the rest of her days—starting at age sixteen—on welfare.

Little Joe, age thirteen, already has a record, a blemish he will never be able to shake, that will always stand in the way of an honest living. And if a boy or a man can't make a living honestly, well . . . there are other ways . . .

Three young people. Three missteps, which neither their meager years nor their more meager backgrounds equipped them to avoid. Three young people, crippled by their environments: for John Ash, a cooped-up basement apartment; for Little Joe, a fifth-floor, roach-infested apartment with a "shooting gallery" outside the door; for Cora, a tenement filled with pregnant teenagers on a street loaded with junkies and pimps.

Three young people. Three missteps. Three scars for a lifetime.

portfolio:

poverty's

playground

you can't fight city hall

A MOTHER walks into a bedroom to find her baby being bitten by a rat; when the mother approaches, the rat attacks her . . . a housewife looks up to find a rat wedged in a hole in the kitchen ceiling; she calls in a cop; he refuses to touch it . . . a grandmother's orphaned grand-daughter is confined in a state institution because in the atmosphere of her rat-plagued apartment, the child's attacks of asthma quickly return . . . during a TV newscast on slum conditions, a daughter turns to her mother and asks, "Mama, we don't live in a house like that, do we?"; at precisely that moment, there is a crash from behind a door; the bath-room ceiling has just fallen in . . . a family is driven out of its apart-ment in the middle of winter when water from a broken upstairs pipe floods the kitchen . . . a woman's leg is scarred by bites from "them big black water bugs" . . .

In dead of winter, with no heat in the house, dangerous electric heaters share the children's sleeping room . . . trash and garbage lie uncollected in the halls . . . and there is the omnipresent, penetrating stench of urine.

These are some of the manifold horrors of slum living. They were all actually observed during no more than half-a -dozen excursions into the blight of just two cities (New York and Washington).

How does a slum tenant combat these affronts to decency? Does he appeal to the landlord? Does he move out? (Move where? At the rent he can afford, he's lucky to have a roof over his head—and he and his landlord both know it.)

But at least there's a housing law. These outrages must be against the law.

And so the tenant turns to his last hope: the city's code enforcers. If they can't help him, no one can.

January 2. Dead of winter. Call it C-Day (for Complaint)—the first day Alice Randall calls the city Buildings Department to see if *they* won't help get her apartment fixed. For most of the nine years she's been living in her building, she's been trying to get the landlord to do something about the ceilings, which now sag ominously in three of her four rooms. Out in the hall, the skylight is broken. There are serious water leaks in her apartment.

Now Alice is turning to the city for help. A clerk takes the information. "Potentially hazardous," he writes on the complaint form.

Mrs. Randall, a widow with two sons, waits to hear from the Buildings Department. Forty days of winter pass. The roof continues to leak. The ceilings bow deeper.

February 11. C plus forty. At last, an envelope from the Buildings Department. Contents: one pink form. RETURN THIS FORM IN THIRTY DAYS, it says, IF THE NEEDED REPAIRS HAVE NOT BEEN MADE. The ceilings still buckle. The roof still leaks.

February 19. A Buildings Department inspector visits Mrs. Randall's building. He inspects the first floor, the second floor and the cellar, but not her fifth-floor apartment. She is unaware of his visit; he is unaware of her complaint, lodged one month and seventeen days ago.

March 5. C plus two months, three days. Another envelope from the Buildings Department. *Another* pink form. RETURN IN 30 DAYS IF . . .

March 7. Mrs. Randall returns the first pink slip to the Department. March 18. Her son jams a large piece of plywood into the skylight to try to keep the rain out.

March 25 (C plus two months, twenty-three days): the bedroom ceiling falls. The bathroom ceiling continues to buckle threateningly. From the Buildings Department: silence.

April 5. Mrs. Randall returns the second pink form. In the apartment just below hers that day, unbeknownst to her, another inspector —this one from the Health Department—also unaware of her months-old complaint, is inspecting for rats.

May 7. Four months and five days after her first appeal for help, a Buildings Department inspector responds. He finds thirteen violations in her building, four of them in the Randall apartment alone.

At last, action. Violations have been found. Now the landlord can be brought into court. The matter is dispatched to the Violations Section.

October 25. Autumn has arrived, but as yet, a summons has not even been served on the landlord in the Alice Randall case. Why not? The city process servers cannot locate the landlord. Yet, a group of volunteer ladies working on the case find him quite easily: simply by going to the building on a day the tenants say their rent is to be collected.

Late November. Winter again descends on the city. The missing landlord is found. A summons is served.

December 27. It is now six days short of a year since Mrs. Randall first complained about the "potentially hazardous" conditions in her apartment. Her landlord is brought into court. He is duly found guilty of the thirteen violations in the Randall building, four of them in the Randall apartment.

The sentence: Correct the violations and pay sixty-five dollars in fines (five dollars per violation).

Five dollars fine for a sagging ceiling that finally fell. Five dollars for a broken skylight that let in the rain.

For her four rooms, Mrs. Randall pays $70 rent. In the nine years she has lived in that apartment, she has paid the landlord $7,560. In the year (less six days) that has elapsed since she first appealed to the city for help, she has paid him $840. The fine for the four violations in her apartment: $20.

There are sixteen apartments in Mrs. Randall's building. Total rent collections in a year: more than thirteen thousand dollars. Fines levied for thirteen violations: sixty-five dollars.

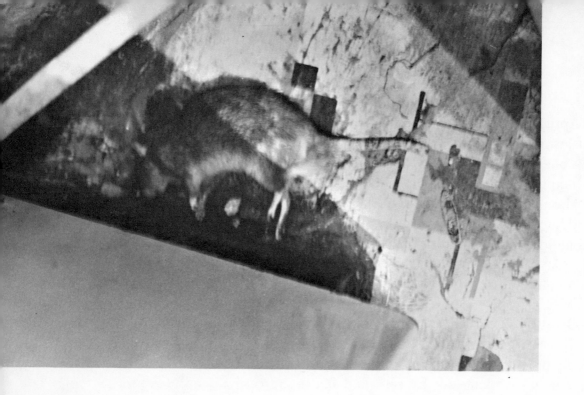

There is not one word of fiction in the chronicle of Alice Randall's year-long struggle for help from the city. It is true in every detail. It is also typical. Even so, it does not tell the whole story.

It omits, for example, the violations found in her building (but not enforced) in forty-six separate inspections—by three separate city departments—in the three years *prior* to Mrs. Randall's complaint.

Also, Mrs. Randall was lucky enough to reach the correct department on her first call. But what if her complaint had involved water in her house? There are eighteen different varieties of water complaints that can be lodged with the city. Depending on their nature, they might go to any one of *four* city departments. If the water in question is rusty but not contaminated, for instance, the complaint goes to the Buildings Department. If, however the water is contaminated, but not rusty, the Buildings Department can't handle it. Kindly call the Health Department. If a welfare worker sees a rat, crawling over the floor, he is instructed to report this to the Buildings Department. But, if he sees the rat actually biting a child, he is to report this to the Health Department.

But the heart of the matter lies elsewhere. Even if the cities' enforcement machinery were reformed into models of efficiency, simplicity and honesty, this would not alter the crucial fact that Alice Randall's tenement and tens of thousands just like it are suffering from exhaustion. They are the residue of decades of decay, abuse, neglect. Most of these ancient structures are too old, too tired to be repaired, even if the landlord wanted, or was forced to restore them. A plaster patch in a broken ceiling of this vintage is an ephemeral thing. It will cling there for a while, Damoclean fashion, until the kids upstairs have their first scuffle. Clamp a leaking and corroded pipe here and the water will soon break out somewhere else.

The fact is that most of these buildings shouldn't even be in use. They deserved an honorable retirement years ago.

But society won't let them retire, for it refuses to provide successors. In 1964, a million and a half new homes were built in America. Less than one and a half per cent of these were for people of low income. In that year, the twenty-fifth anniversary of public housing, low-rent government units still standing in this country constituted just one per cent of the nation's housing.

If anything, the supply of low-income housing is shrinking. Multi-lane expressways (wholly useless to the carless poor) and gleaming urban renewals projects have devoured many slums and dispossessed their residents. Their evacuees are seeking refuge and shelter in the only places that they can afford: the already run-down, already over-crowded pockets of blight elsewhere in the city; and, as basements become even more crammed with humanity, the law of supply and demand drives up the price of squalid living.

And so, Alice Randall's tenement, and tens of thousands of other exhausted buildings, continue to be pressed into service far, far beyond their natural lives. So long as this is true, Alice Randall and thousands of others like her will be sentenced to fight a losing battle with code enforcers, with the landlords—and with rats that bite, roaches that crawl, ceilings that buckle and fall, and roofs that let in the rain.

"we can't help him,

he's too poor"

JOHN WILSON of Washington, D. C. lived within a few blocks of embassies and grand houses. But his house was not grand: it consisted of a single room, ten by fifteen feet—home for John, his wife and five of his ten children (the other five had to be boarded with an aunt). The room cost him $65 a month.

John worked as a dishwasher in a downtown hotel—an occupation yet to be reached by the minimum wage law that has been on the United States statute books for twenty-five years. His work week: six days. Pay: $57.

John Wilson's home was not grand—it consisted of a single room, ten by fifteen.

Every Saturday he took home $53—and paid $15 of it to his landlord.

John had a wish. He wanted to get his ten children back under one roof. Not an unreasonable wish. At one point they had all been together, crammed into two rooms, with the side use of a kitchen and a bath (cost: $35 a week—$152 a month). But then the landlord counted the children—nine, then, and a tenth on the way—and had thrown him out.

His one hope lay in public housing. A poor man, he was told, could get a large enough apartment for $45 a month. He applied. For a long time, no answer. Then a form-letter reply:

> "We regret to inform you that, after careful exami-
> nation of the facts presented in your application, we
> have found you to be ineligible for the following
> reasons . . . (and in ink below) INSUFFICIENT
> FUNDS."

The judgment: John Wilson was too poor to pay $45 a month for a six-bedroom apartment. *The sentence:* John Wilson must continue paying $65 a month, half again as much, for a single room inadequate to house even half of his children.

But the story does not end there. When the situation was brought to light by the *Washington Post*, public housing officials said they had been misunderstood. John Wilson, they explained, wasn't exactly ineligible. It was just that there weren't any apartments for people with such low incomes. But they would put him on the waiting list. Along with 6,000 other families. There are only four vacancies a year in the six-bedroom category. There are a hundred and one applicants for six-bedroom apartments. Even with a top priority rating, officials said it would take John Wilson six years to get an apartment.

At the time this occurred (late 1963) in the capital of the richest nation in the world, not one public housing unit had been built for nearly three years.

108

no hidin' place

You walk up a flight of stairs. At the head of the stairs, tacked to the tired, broken plaster, an imitation sampler:

A TRUE FRIEND

IS A RARE TREASURE

Past the sampler, two small rooms, over an abandoned corner store. Window panes broken or missing. Every faucet leaks. Stove burners clogged and useless. Oven door half off. There, with just two beds and two extra mattresses among them, lives the Fletcher family: three adults, nine children.

The law does not permit twelve people to live in two rooms. Illegal overcrowding. If an inspector knew about this, he'd throw them out.

But the new owner of the store and apartment wants them out anyway. He has shut off the heat, and winter is coming in fast. He has given them until Saturday to move out.

Where to go? There simply are no places in the city that will take nine children—not, at any rate, in the Fletcher's price range. The Fletchers know there aren't. They've been looking for months, following every lead, ready to grasp at anything, *anything* just as most people in the country were doing in the terrible wartime and postwar housing shortage.

They had been living in a run-down house a few blocks away— so run-down that it was condemned by the city as "unfit for human

habitation." On the day they were to be evicted Mr. Fletcher heard about the two rooms above the store. How many children do you have? Three. Okay. Seventy-five a month (for two rooms!). One month's rent in advance.

They scraped up the seventy-five dollars and moved in. Now they have to move out.

Where to go? Public housing? That would seem the logical place for a poor family with lots of children. But no. The doors there are closed to this family. Reason: Mrs. Fletcher's legal husband, now a mental patient in a veterans' hospital, has refused to give her a divorce. A lawyer *might* be able to wangle one for her, but that would cost two hundred dollars—maybe more. (Legal Aid won't handle divorce cases unless there are no illegitimate children involved.) Her relationship with Mr. Fletcher is as stable and solid as any marriage (ninth anniversary coming up this February). But the laws says it is no marriage, and so society shuts its eyes to need and bars the public housing doors to Mrs. Fletcher and her nine children.

Move by Saturday, the landlord says. But where? The family doesn't know the answer. The social worker in charge of their case doesn't know, either. She is sympathetic and worried. But she can't work magic and produce a house where none exists.

What is to happen to them? If they are lucky, they'll find another place and lie again about the number of children and wedge themselves into another forbidden room or two until a neighbor reports them and the law or the landlord forces them out.

If they are unlucky, they'll be set out on the street. The Women's Bureau will take in the parents and the kids will go to the city's shelter for homeless children. It costs about $3,600 a year to keep a child in that shelter. The nine Fletcher children will cost the city $32,500 a year. $32,500. Enough to buy a house for the Fletchers, or pay their rent for several years.

"For want of a horseshoe nail, the battle was lost." For want of a house, a family was lost.

You stand at the top of the stairs above the abandoned corner store. Children race about noisily. Is there *no one*, you wonder, in this entire city—no one in this capital of the richest nation in the world, who can help find a legal, decent shelter for these nine children and their parents?

You wonder. But there is no answer.

When the Fletchers move out of their unheated two rooms to God-knows-where, they will take with them the imitation sampler at the top of the stairs:

A TRUE FRIEND

IS A RARE TREASURE

portfolio:

american

madonnas

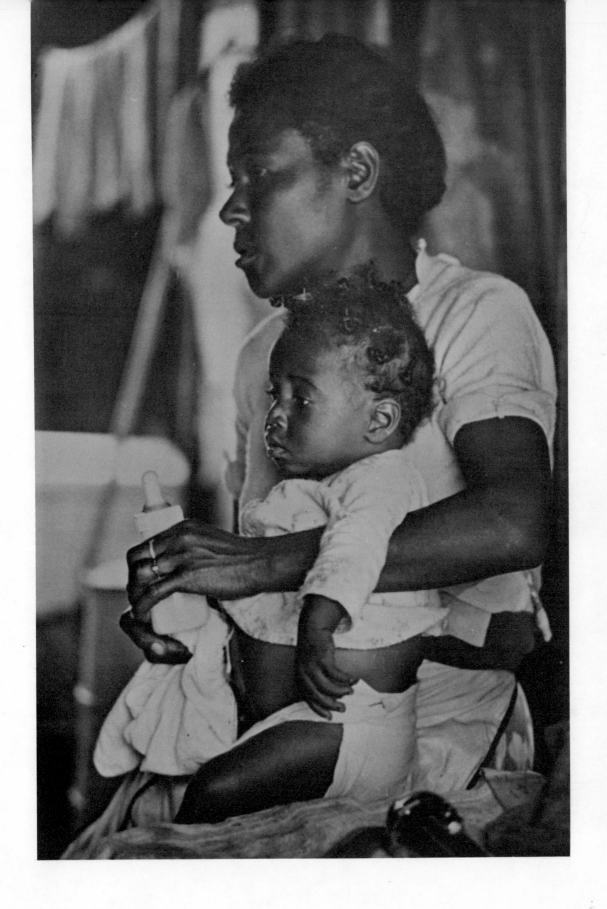

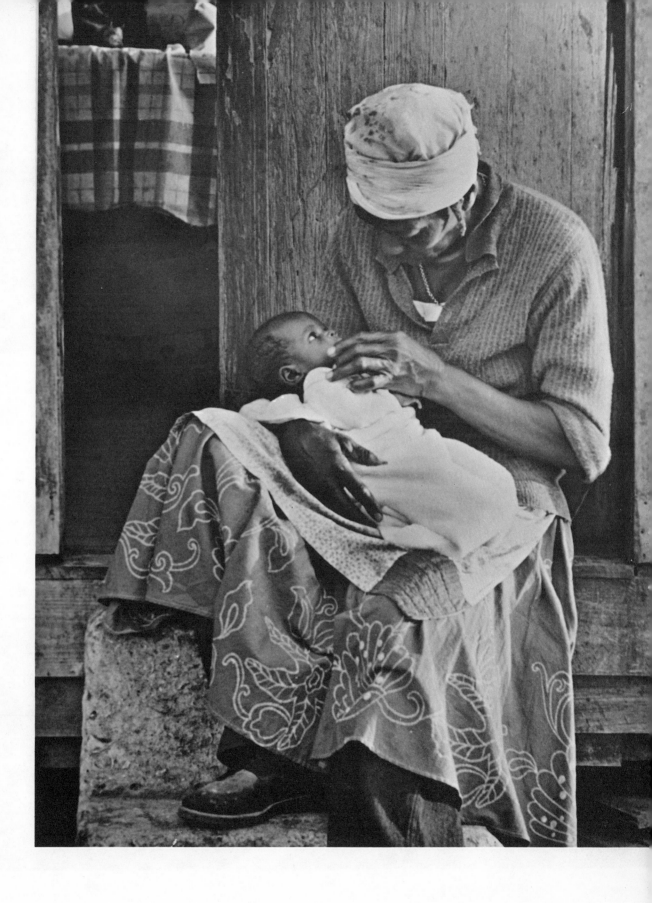

imbalance

THIS is South Phoenix, Arizona. Seeing these shacks for the first time, you are sure no one lives in them; they must be abandoned. But, you find, people do live in them. Few of them own cars.

Not a hundred feet away from these shacks stands a six-lane elevated expressway. For those who own cars and have a pleasant or profitable place to go, it will save five minutes, maybe ten, in traveling through Phoenix. It cost a million dollars a mile. It is of no use to a person who doesn't own a car.

In 1963 the Federal government spent two and a half billion dollars building expressways like this one. It spent less than one-tenth that amount building decent houses for people who live in shacks and slums.

whose welfare state?

Place: MISSISSIPPI. Year: 1964. Average grant to feed, clothe and house the average child in a breadwinnerless family: less than 32 cents a day.

Place: Florida. *Year:* 1964. Minimum *need* for a family of four (according to the state welfare department): $106.81 per month. *Actual* welfare grant to such a family: $60.45. About 52 cents per person per day for food, clothing and shelter. Average medical benefit for such a family of four: $1.57 per month.

Place: Florida. *Year:* 1964. Minimum welfare grant that may be made under the law, no matter how large the family: $81 per month. Per-person survival money for a family of twelve: less than 25 cents a day.

Place: Chicago. *Year:* 1962. Clothing allowance for children two through six: one sweater and three union suits every *three* years; one underskirt, two pants and one flannel sleeper and one cotton sleeper *per year*.

Place: United States of America. Richest country in the world. *Year:* 1964. National average per-person welfare grant for food, clothing and shelter: one dollar a day. For a family of five: $35 a week.

Place: United States of America. *Year:* 1962. Tax subsidy to the Humble Oil Company (Esso); over $440 million—nearly half a billion dollars. Tax subsidy to Continental Oil Company: over $35 million. Tax subsidy to The Getty Oil Company (79 per cent owned by J. Paul Getty, reportedly the richest man in the nation): over $5 million.

Place: United States of America. *Year:* 1964. Average social security old-age payment: $29 per week.

Place: United States of America. *Year:* 1964. Average unemployment benefit paid: $35 a week (one dollar per person per day for a family of five). Maximum duration of benefits: twenty-six weeks. Number of men who exhausted their benefits and were without income: nearly a million and a half.

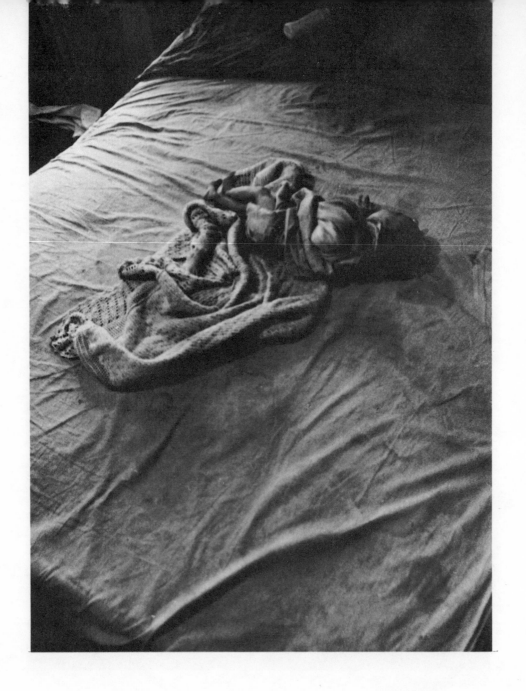

Place: Alabama. *Year:* 1964. Maximum an unemployed man can get in jobless benefits: $32 a week. *Actual average* jobless benefit: $26 per week.

Place: United States of America. *Year:* 1960.
Postal subsidy to *Life Magazine:* nearly $10 million.
Postal subsidy to the *Reader's Digest:* nearly $5 million.

124

Place: Washington, D. C.—capital of the richest nation in the world. *Year:* 1964. Maximum allowance for rent and all utilities for welfare "clients" (set in 1953, unchanged since then): $76 a month. Per cent of welfare recipients able to find shelter for $76 a month: virtually zero. Per cent dipping into food and clothing allowances to pay the rent: virtually 100. Food allowance to be dipped into (based on 1957 Agriculture bare-subsistence budget)—for a family of twelve: seventeen and a half cents per person per meal. Clothing allowance for such a family: five dollars per person per month. Allowance for "personal household needs" for a family of twelve: two dollars per person per month.

Place: Fresno County, California. *Year:* 1961. Cotton subsidy to one farm: $1,551,462.
Place: Maricopa County, Arizona. *Year:* 1961. Cotton subsidy to farm owned by Arizona Title and Insurance Company and Del E. Webb Development Company: $560,000.

Place: United States of America. *Years:* 1952-61. Number of new homes built in the decade: a billion and a quarter. Number built for low-income slum dwellers: less than three hundred thousand—about two per cent of the total. Administration's public housing program (as of 1964) to build 35,000 units per year for four years. Number of slum dwellers who could be housed by such a program: one in eighty. Total Federal expenditures for public housing, 1963: $195 million.

Place: United States of America. *Year:* 1963. Shipbuilding subsidy to five companies: $110 million. Subsidy to the Grace Line: nearly $30 million; to the U. S. Lines: $26,564,000.

"but we can't afford

to help the poor"

Place: WASHINGTON. *Scene:* Congress of the United States. Resolved: The United States of America will put a man on the moon before 1970. Cost: $20 billion. All in favor say aye. Carried overwhelmingly.

Can we afford the $20 billion?

Certainly

> *Place:* Washington. *Scene:* Emergency Room of D. C. General Hospital, twenty blocks from where Congress meets. Indigent patients are waiting to see a doctor. Average waiting time: three to six hours; at times, up to twelve hours of waiting. Main reason: not enough staff. Cost of staffing the Emergency Room properly: about $180,000.

Can we afford the $180,000? Apparently not.

Place: Washington. *Scene:* U.S. House of Representatives. Resolved: Congress should appropriate one and a half billion dollars for the construction of new military camps and bases. You have heard the two hours of debate on this billion-dollar question, gentlemen. Are you ready to vote? In favor: 340. Opposed: 5.

Can we afford the billion and a half?

Unquestionably.

> *Place:* Washington. *Scene:* A playground, not more than fifteen blocks from where the House of Representatives meets. Time: A sunny, warm Sunday in February. A hundred city kids mill around outside the park. They can't get in. It's closed this Sunday. Reason: lack of funds. Cost of opening it that day: $110.

Can we afford the $110?

Apparently not.

> *Place:* Washington. *Scene:* The Congress. Resolved: There shall be authorized the spending of $2.3 billion for the dredging of rivers and harbors and for beach erosion projects. Shouted through the House by voice vote, October 3, 1962. Shouted through the Senate by voice vote, October 4, 1962.

Can we afford the $2.3 billion?

Indubitably.

> *Place:* Washington. *Scene:* The Ludlow Elementary School, eighteen blocks from where Congress meets. Built in 1903, the Ludlow School has no washbasins in the lavatories. In fact, there is only one washbasin for 260 children. There are no definite plans for building a new school to replace Ludlow.

> *Place:* Washington. *Scene:* Harrison Elementary School, twenty-five blocks from the Capitol. Built in 1890, Harrison has no auditorium. Assemblies must be held in the corridor, in violation of fire regulations. There are no definite plans to replace Harrison school.

Place: Washington. *Scene:* Shaw Junior High School, twenty blocks from the Capitol. Built in 1903, its replacement was recommended in 1948.

Seventeen years later, it is still in use—by 300 more children than it is supposed to hold. Classes are held in converted locker rooms and converted storerooms. The earliest it can be replaced is 1968.

Can we afford to replace these ancient schools with new ones?

Maybe soon. But, apparently, not now. Rivers and harbors first. Schools second.

Scene: Washington. *Time:* Summer, 1961. The Berlin crisis heats up. The President of the United States talks to the nation via television. Three and a half billion more dollars needed for America's and the free world's defense. Congress' reaction: By all means. Defense spending must be supported. (Of course, *domestic* spending will have to be cut back to make up for the defense increase. Naturally, there will have to be cuts in programs like low-rent public housing.)

Berlin is, of course, a crisis. An emergency.

What about 600 rat bites a year in the city of New York?

That's no crisis. It's an annual event.

What about the hundreds of families crammed into basements in Washington, D. C.?

That's no emergency. It's been that way for years.

We'll have to cut back on the housing program. Those non-emergencies will have to wait.

A national imperative: to maintain the highest quality among the men and women of our armed forces.

Price tag of that imperative: nearly $3 billion (in military pay increases voted in the last ten years)— enough to give every teacher in the United States a $2,000 yearly pay raise.

All Congressmen in favor: 293. Opposed: 10. All Senators in favor: 94. Opposed: none.

Can we afford the $3 billion? Without question.

> In Perry County, Kentucky, in the heart of stricken Appalachia, where the last hope of children's escape from permanent poverty and dependency is a first-rate education, one-fifth of the teachers have only "emergency" certificates—which means they do not even have a bachelor's degree.

> A prime reason: Low teacher pay. Starting salary: $3,870 a year. On an annual basis, that comes to just $74.42 a week.

> If a person follows a career of teaching in Perry County, Kentucky, he can hope, one day, to make $94.42 a week. No more.

We can afford to make sure we get the best to wield the instruments of death and destruction.

Can we afford to make sure we get the best to wield the tools of knowledge?

Apparently not.

the price

of our failures

AMERICA is a cost-minded, price-minded nation. It prides itself on avoiding waste; on getting the most for our money; on asking, "How much does it cost? What's the price?"

Except, perhaps, when it comes to the cost, the waste, the price of poverty.

America tolerates blight in its cities.
And it pays for it.
For blight is hoggish with the taxpayer's dollar.

Blight in New York City: Blighted areas contain 27 per cent of the city's population . . . yet account for 45 per cent of the city's infant deaths, 71 per cent of the venereal disease, 51 per cent of the juvenile delinquency, 73 per cent of the dependent-children-on-welfare.

Blight in Sacramento: Blighted areas contain 20 per cent of the population . . . yet account for 42 per cent of the city's adult crime . . . and 41 per cent of the police and fire costs. Twenty per cent of the population . . . yet the blighted areas account for 76 per cent of the city's tuberculosis . . . eat up 50 per cent of the city's health budget.

Blight in Los Angeles: For every tax dollar collected from a "good" area, only 38 cents are paid in by blighted areas . . . yet for every dollar spent in the "good" area blight sucks in $1.87 for police, $1.67 for fire, $2.25 for health.

Blight in Newark: every dwelling in the blighted areas *costs* the city $380 more than it pays in taxes . . . while in a "good" area, every dwelling *pays in* $420 more than it gets in services.

For the failures in its educational system, America pays many prices. The draft is just one.

One out of every four eighteen-year-old draftees is too poorly educated to serve in his country's armed forces. That is, at age eighteen, he cannot do *eighth* grade work.

Four out of five of these boys are school dropouts. One in three comes from a broken family. One in eight comes from a welfare family.

Where one young man is too poorly educated to serve his country, another young man—a better educated young man—must take his place.

Poverty fosters dope addiction.
And there's a price to be paid.

The average dope addict has to beg, borrow, or, most often, steal $50,000 worth of property a year to get enough cash to feed his habit.

Poverty fosters dope addiction.
And America pays for it.

The United States underpays and overloads its social workers —a hundred and fifty cases, two hundred, sometimes three hundred. They are check-writers at best, cops at worst, but rarely problem-solvers. They fail too often to get at the root problems of welfare "clients." Few are helped to get off the dole; more get on; the costs rise. Ten years ago America was paying $2½ billion in welfare. Today it is paying nearly $5 billion.

This country fails to get at the root problems of its welfare "clients."

And it pays for it.

It costs $13,000 to raise and educate an unwanted, unintended child who becomes a ward of the city or state.

It costs just $30 a year to give birth control services to one potential mother.

For every $30 saved the taxpayers by failing to give birth control services, there is a risk of costing the taxpayers $13,000.

That is, for every dollar saved, there is a risk of losing $433.

Often measures are not taken that could keep a family together. Sometimes welfare laws even *encourage* family split-ups.

And this must be paid for.

A dependent child on welfare costs the taxpayers $390 a year.

A child in a united, self-supporting family costs the taxpayers nothing.

Often measures are not taken that could keep a child with its mother. Simple measures—such as providing them a decent roof over their heads. And this must be paid for.

A child in a foster home costs the taxpayers about $1,200 a year.

A child in an institution costs the taxpayers from $2,000 to $9,000 a year.

A child in a united, self-supporting family costs the taxpayers nothing.

hurdles

You're talking with Doris Walker. Age: Fifteen. Dropped out of school to have a baby.

"You've just got to go back to school, Doris. You'll never make it if you don't have an education."

Good advice. Easy to say. Not so easy to do. Not so easy to leave that new baby and go back to school with the thirteen-year-olds and be razzed and begin again on a school year you almost finished but not quite.

Easy to say. Not so easy to do.

You're talking with Darell Graves,* unemployed ex-coal miner, in the hills of Kentucky.

"Why don't you sign up with that training program in town and learn a new trade? There's sure no future in mining."

Easy advice, easily given. But Darell's shack is fourteen miles from town, two miles up a "holler" from the main road. *You* drove up to see Darell in your rented car (and even at that it was a half hour from town). But Darell has no car. For him, the training course would mean starting out before dawn, walking the two miles to the main road, and taking the bus to town. And back in the afternoon. Two, two and a half hours a day traveling. Not easy. But do-able.

Except who's going to pay for the bus fare? And for his lunch in town (the training course pays for neither)? Remember, Darell is trying to keep a wife and seven kids alive on twenty dollars a month.

* See p. 19.

133

And even if he could manage, somehow, to swing bus fare and lunch, would it be worth it? What kind of job would there be for Darell in this God-forsaken job-forsaken part of the world?

"Well, if you learned a trade, you could move somewhere else and get a job."

Another easily-formed, easily-uttered collection of words. But Darell Graves grew up in these hills; he's never left them. To him The City is just one big frightening question mark. Move where? To what kind of a job? To what kind of a house? To what friends? And where is he to get the money to travel and move his family? Strike out on his own and bring the family later? Possible. But frightening for a man his age, to pick up and start all over again in strange, alien surroundings. And there's that first question: Move *where?* A man doesn't just close his eyes and plunk his finger down on a map. Before he ventures out, a man wants to have some friends, some connections. And a little money. Darell Graves has none of those things.

The whole thing *is* do-able—the getting up before dawn, the bus to town, the training course, even the uprooting and moving to God-knows-where. Yes, do-able—but not by a man of just average courage, average ambition, average hope. A man needs an extra endowment of all three if he's going to clear the hurdles of being ill-educated, provincial—and poor.

"The trouble with these goddam people on welfare—and it's the same with these kids, too—is that they'd rather sit on their asses than go to work. They ought to get off their butts and get a job."

Easy enough to say. Not so easy if . . .

If, for instance, you can't read and write well enough to do fifth grade work.* Technically, you're "able-bodied." But educationally, in a job market like Chicago, you're a cripple.

Or if you're a kid who's rarely been out of Harlem, who's lost in downtown Manhattan (and who wants a messenger who can't find his way around?), who doesn't own a necktie and whose mother doesn't know how—or has no place—to iron a shirt.

Or if you're a Negro farm girl in broken-down sneakers and a torn dress standing awkwardly by your shabby farmhouse near Col-

* This was true of half the welfare recipients surveyed in South Chicago. See p. 141.

"If you can't read the signs, how you gonna know which way to go?"

"I'd rather miss a couple days' eatin' and have all the learnin' in the world than to have none 'tall."

umbia, S. C., a fresh high school diploma in your hand (A's and B's in typing), but without the remotest notion of how to dress or groom yourself for even the lowliest typist's job in the city.

Or let's say you're Bob Hunter, city boy of eighteen with a chance for a construction job way out in the suburbs. Not so simple: make your way out to the country for a job interview; back out again another day to pick up the application for a minor's work permit; back to the boss to get him to sign it; find a doctor to give you a medical okay (how? you don't know any doctors); the first doctor you find can't see you for a week; the second can give you an appointment, all right, but his office is half way to the next city. You get through all that; the job's yours—but first you've got to line yourself up a way to get to and from work every day (the buses don't run out that far).

All told, an obstacle course that takes four days and four hundred miles of driving—all for a seasonal, no-work-when-it-rains construction job.

Most kids of eighteen wouldn't complete the obstacle course. They'd give up. You're lucky. The social worker who's been working with your gang spends the four days and drives the four hundred miles to make sure you and the job get together. But what about the thousands of Bob Hunters who have nobody like that to lead them through the obstacle course?

You're Willie Morrison, one of the thousands of unemployed Negroes in your city—out of work, now, for nearly six months. But now you've got a chance. Through a friend, a contractor decides to give you a try. Show up Tuesday morning—seven o'clock.

But Monday night you get word the landlord is going to throw you out of your house next day because you're behind on your rent. It took you four months to find that house—Lord knows when you'd find another. So you stay home Tuesday to fight off the landlord and try to keep a roof over your family's head.

When you show up Wednesday, your job's been filled. Good-bye, job.

Sometimes poverty—sheer lack of money—creates its own hurdles.

As, for example, with Frank Gillis, a South Carolina farmer who can't afford to buy tested cotton seed, buys untested, cut-rate seed instead, and doesn't discover until summer, when half the crop fails to come up, that the seed was no good. But by then it's too late.

Or as with Mamie, one of Frank's hard-pressed neighbors, who is just about wiped out by drought. Not her prosperous white neighbor, though. The drought won't wipe him out. He keeps his crop alive with tank trucks that water his fields.

Or as with John Patterson in Arkansas,* who has to thin out his cotton rows, for want of fertilizer, and let some of his land go untilled for want of machinery to clear it and tractor to plow it.

Or as with Ivan Young Bear, sitting idle on a parched Indian reservation in Arizona, while white men, able to outbid most of the Indians for the leases, farm the best of the precious water-fed land.

Or as with Willie Johnson, ex-coal miner trapped in the hills of West Virginia with a wife and eight children, living (or at any rate surviving) on an unstretchable welfare check that provides precisely fourteen and a half cents per person per meal—provided they don't buy anything else. But a family has to buy other things. Four of the children need shoes to stay in school. Which shoes to buy— the four-dollars cardboard-like kind (which will mean doing without 110 meals that month) or the eight-dollar variety that will last far

* See p. 29.

137

more than twice as long (but will also mean forgoing 220 meals)? It's shoes versus food. The choice is cruel, clear—and, in the long run, far more expensive. Four pairs of four-dollar shoes, please.

Even if you're not faced with the desperation of a shoes-versus-food choice, chances are you are caught in a vise reserved for the poor—a vise that squeezes from both sides: you get less, but you pay more.

More, for example, for rent.

Take Washington, D. C. In the suburbs, four-room apartments can be had, the newspaper says, for $84.50 a month. In the heart of a Washington slum, Mrs. Ruth Lamberton pays $98 a month. But she doesn't get four rooms. She gets two. And the two don't include a bath. That's in the hall, to be shared.

Even in the city, just a few dollars more than Mrs. Lamberton is paying will rent three rooms, complete (the ad says) with "AIR CONDITIONING, SWIMMING POOL AND PLAY AREAS." But the price there does not include the privilege of illegally cramming herself and seven children into two rooms, as she does in the slums. Mrs. Lamberton is paying a premium for being allowed to break the law. (To be more precise, her *children* are paying the premium, since her welfare check only includes $76 for rent—$22 less than she is paying for her two rooms. The difference comes out of the food budget.)

When the Mrs. Lambertons of this world buy a new washing machine or TV, they are not likely to venture into inaccessible, unfriendly and bewildering "downtown." Chances are they get it from a fast-talking door-to-door salesman, or from a friendly neighborhood appliance store, always willing if not eager to sell a shoddy, off-brand machine on easy terms (no money down, plenty of time to pay)—but at a price. Somebody has to pay the price for the risk he takes. Mrs. Lamberton pays. So do her neighbors.

There are other hurdles.

Language, for example. Frank Ramirez is a Mexican-American who somehow manages to shoehorn his family of nine into a one-room shack near Phoenix. His crippled English bars him from doing

On his sixteenth birthday, he didn't say aye, yes or no. He just picked up his books and quit school.

If a person's skin is black, the catalogue of disadvantages is long and increasingly familiar.

anything more exalted or remunerative than pruning grapes or cleaning onions for four or five dollars per twelve-hour day.

Or poor health. For a man who lives in a tenement where there's often no heat for weeks at a time in the coldest part of winter, who has no family doctor, for whom the city hospital is three bus-transfers across town, sickness is likely to be a frequent and tenacious visitor. When a man is sick he can't work; when he doesn't work he doesn't get paid, and medical care becomes even more remote. And so the downward spiral gains momentum.

Or the color of a man's skin. If it's black, the catalogue of disadvantages and barriers is long and increasingly familiar. With a black skin a man is four times as likely to be on welfare, twice as likely to be jobless. Even if he has a job, he will, typically, earn about a sixth less than if his skin were white.

He'll earn less, but often he'll pay more. In Buffalo, New York, white urban renewal dislocatees typically paid $48.79 in rent. Negro dislocatees, with a thousand dollars less income, on the average, paid

$64.61—a third more. In Chicago, white welfare recipients typically pay $64.84 rent, Negroes $82.77.

Thus society sets up higher hurdles for the poor, and at the same time denies them the wherewithal to clear them: a decent education.

Of welfare recipients in South Chicago, more than 90 per cent had finished more than five years' schooling; yet half could not read or write well enough to do fifth-grade work.

"You try to move a little faster, so the world won't leave you behind with your head in your hands."

Of those educated in rural Mississippi, four-fifths had gone beyond the fifth grade; yet only one out of four could perform fifth-grade work.

Mississippi has the lowest per-person income of all the states. It also spends the least per child for schools ($241 compared with New York's $705). It also pays the lowest teachers' salaries.

Only half as much is spent on the education of a slum child as on a suburban child.

In half of all poor families, the head of the household has had less than an eighth-grade education.

Herein lies the root cause of American poverty. Herein lie the seeds of the poverty of the future.

he who needs the most help

gets the least

A VACANCY opens up in a public housing project. Who will get it? John Wilson and his ten children—the family that was "too poor to be helped?" * Or the Rosses and their nine children, taking refuge in a basement furnace room? **

Not likely. Apartments for a nine- or ten-children family are the scarcest in public housing projects. This new vacancy is a two-bedroom apartment, just right for a two-child family (the kind that has the easiest time finding a place on the private market). For the Wilsons and the Rosses, the waiting time is the longest. They'll be the last to get into public housing.

* See p. 108.
** See p. 59.

John Wilson is a dishwasher. He puts in six ten-hour days. He gets paid $57. No extra pay for overtime.

Across town is another John—John Dresinski, skilled machinist. His pay: $3.82 an hour—$152.80 for a straight-time 40-hour week. For any work beyond 40 hours, time and a half—$5.73 an hour.

John Dresinski is covered by the Federal minimum wage. John Wilson is not.

For Esther Cook, migrant mother of four, only one day out of two offers a chance to work. For half of every year, she's idle.

John Dresinski has been laid off a little less than four weeks in the past four years.

During his idle week-a-year, John Dresinski gets $53 in the form of unemployment compensation.

During *her* idle six months a year, Esther Cook gets no pay at all—zero.

John Dresinski, machinist, highly skilled and highly paid, is comfortably cushioned not only against unemployment but against old age as well. A steady earner of top wages, his jobless benefits are as high as they come. So, too, his social security benefits when he retires.

John Wilson, dishwasher, is also covered by social security. But he is unskilled, low-paid, and a sporadic job-holder, the first to be laid off when a business boom fades. His social security benefits will be minimal—probably around $15 a week. He will be among America's aged paupers.

So will Esther Cook. She doesn't work long enough for any one employer to be covered by social security.

So will John Patterson,* Ozark farmer. He applied for social security. But he doesn't have enough cash income to qualify.

Suppose John Dresinski's employer falls on hard times and goes out of business. Suppose, too, that John Wilson is laid off from his dishwashing job. Both seek help from USES—the United States Employment Service. Congressional appropriations for USES are

* See p. 29.

based, in part, on the number of men it *succeeds* in placing in jobs. Failures are a black mark; they make the monthly report look bad.

Who is likely to get the priority attention at USES—skilled, easy-to-place John Dresinski? Or unskilled John Wilson, common dishwasher?

Skill. That's what John Wilson needs. Training. The government has a program for that. John Wilson applies. There are a thousand applicants for a hundred openings in the school. How far did you get in school, Wilson? Third grade? Sorry, this class requires a tenth-grade education. We'll call you as soon as we have something for you. Next man, please.

Some cities permit social workers to refer welfare "clients" to birth control clinics. But which clients? Would a worker be permitted to mention the subject to Cora,* the 16-year-old ghetto-bound girl whose baby will likely never known a father? Or to Lucille Campbell,* struggling to raise six fatherless children in the slums of Chicago? Or Bea and Daisy,* the two teen-age mothers who are already following in the footsteps of their own husbandless mothers?

No, for such girls, the subject of birth control, the welfare worker's lips are sealed—except to married "clients" who have a legal husband living with them, fathers to help bring up present and future offspring.

APW. Federal alphabetese for "Accelerated Public Works"—a one-time Federal program of building courthouses and armories and the like in "depressed areas" to help create jobs there.

A courthouse is to be built in Whitesburg, Kentucky, in the heart of Appalachia. It takes skilled labor to put up a courthouse. Who will fill the jobs? The Ray Newtons and the Darell Graveses,** whose only trade is sweating coal out of a mountain? No, the job will mostly be done by a skilled crew, imported from already-prosperous Western Kentucky.

(One government official tells of watching a hospital being built on an unemployment-plagued Indian reservation—by imported white

* See p. 90, 55, and 51 respectively.
** See p. 20.

workers who, as they worked and the Indians watched jealously, complained about the "lazy, shiftless Indians.")

Arlington, Virginia, just across the river from Washington, is one of the wealthiest counties in America. Average family income: close to $10,000. Unemployment; virtually nil.

The county has a new, air-conditioned courthouse, an excellent county hospital and, most important, a fine, modern school system. Last year, it turned out ten National Merit Scholars; the year before, eight.

In stark contrast to prosperous Arlington County, Perry County, Kentucky, lies in the heart of the moribund Appalachian coal fields, its people in deep trouble. Unemployment: over 12 per cent (national average: 5 percent). One-sixth of the people are on welfare—many times the national average.

Perry has no county hospital. Its courthouse was once fine, but no longer. On the outside, the paint is peeling; on the inside, the stench of urine from unrepaired toilets is overpowering. But judge not too harshly: per capita income in Perry County is less than a third that of Arlington. The total county budget is $203,000 (Arlington's is $40,000,000—two hundred times as great).

Unless the children of Perry County get a first-rate education, their future will be little less bleak than that of their parents. In many Perry County schools, however, three grades—sometimes five —must share one teacher and one classroom. Per-pupil expenditure in the Perry County schools: $212. Per-pupil expenditure in the Arlington schools: $612.

Teachers in Perry County are paid a little more than half what Arlington teachers receive. Result: one-fifth of them possess only "emergency" teaching certificates—which means they don't even have a bachelor's degree. They do their best to teach three grades, or five, in a single classroom. But it's hard to teach—harder still to concentrate and learn—with three grades in a classroom.

Perry County hasn't turned out a National Merit Scholar for as long as the present school superintendent can remember.

Exactly three and a half miles from the Arlington County Court House, in the heart of one of the cruelest slums in the nation's capi-

Unless the children of Perry County get a first-rate education, their future will be little less bleak than that of their parents.

tal, is the Harrison Elementary school. The people of this Washington slum are in trouble, much as the people of Perry County are. Unemployment and juvenile delinquency are twice as severe as in the city as a whole. Twice as many people are on welfare. Like the children of Perry County, the children of this slum need a first-rate education. Yet one out of every five students enrolled in the nearby high school will become dropouts.

The Harrison School was built in 1890. It has no library. In fact, only fifteen of Washington's hundred and thirty elementary school have any official school library; and those fifteen must share the part-time services of just eight librarians. There is no auditorium at Harrison, so assemblies are held in the hall (in violation of fire regulations). To avoid double shifts, basement rooms are pressed into service as classrooms. The school has just enough modeling clay to permit each class to work in clay twice during the school year. There is no money to take children on bus trips to concerts and museums.

In Arlington County, an elementary school PTA might raise $1,000 during a school year to help make up for such deficiencies. Last year, the Harrison PTA raised a total of $242.86.

Among Arlington's sixth graders, one third have reading skills two years or more *above* the national norm. Less than one in eight is reading below the norm.

At Harrison, though, three-quarters of the sixth graders are reading below grade level; nearly three-fifths are two years or more behind in reading skills.

Expenditures per pupil for the education of Harrison students: about one-half that for Arlington students.

He who needs the most help gets the least.

148

aloneness

A SOCIAL worker takes you to see one of her "clients." Name: Minnie Blake. Mother of four. About to be evicted from her apartment.

You climb three flights of dark stairs, careful not to step on the empty wine bottles. The social worker knocks on the door. It is opened by a barefoot boy of, maybe, seven or eight, wearing nothing but a pair of ripped trousers. His nakedness shows through.

Such furniture as there is is piled up on the side of the room, in preparation for the move. Three older children sit on a bare mattress. At the kitchen table sits Minnie, a large strong woman to whom, you would think, tears would come rarely. But Minnie is in tears.

She is in tears because she is at the end of her rope. She just doesn't know which way to turn, from whom to seek help.

Four days ago her new place was supposed to be ready for her. For four days she's kept the kids home from school to help with the move. For four days she's been told the same thing. Not today, they say; tomorrow it will be ready, but not today. Now it looks as though she may not even get the place at all.

In her pocketbook, the eviction notice. Also, a receipt for twenty dollars—twenty dollars she has been conned out of by an unscrupulous "apartment-finding" company.

She points out the window at the alley that separates her from the next slum building. Bottles, trash, filth. "I'm sick of that alley. They does everything in that alley. This is no place to raise children."

But where is she to go? To whom is she to turn for help?

Aloneness is having no one to join forces with.

Minnie Blake suffers the most cruel and most universal affliction of the poor: aloneness. Not loneliness (although God knows Essie is lonely enough)—aloneness, which is something different.

Aloneness is not knowing which way to turn for help, as with Minnie.

Aloneness is the helplessness of being caught by forces both incomprehensible and uncontrollable, as with Ray Newton, Kentucky miner made obsolete by a machine, reluctant out of pride to resort to the dole, but with no place to turn for a job and for self-respect.

Aloneness is being out of touch, unable to communicate. You see it in the lobby of a dingy pension hotel, lined with men and women sitting soundless, alone, staring at the floor—islands of aloneness. You see it in a lone migrant worker who, in his travels, comes within a short bus ride of his brothers and sisters and his childhood home, but can't bring himself to make the easy trip to see them—afraid they will think him a failure. Even the man in the next chair, even your own brother, is out of reach.

Above all, aloneness is having no one to join forces with, or at any rate not knowing *how* to join forces with other alone people.

Take, for example, Esther Cook, the migrant mother. She suffers substandard wages and subhuman living conditions because she and others like her are unorganized, alone, at the mercy of the market.

Now the growers who employ Esther Cook will tell you that they, too, are at the mercy of the market. And they are. But they do not suffer the migrant's aloneness, for they do not act singly. They band together. Acting together, in Florida, for example, they have softened the harshness of the market's fickleness by forming a marketing agreement so as to act in concert, day by day, on the amount of produce harvested and marketed. Acting together, they have also negotiated the importation of foreign workers, and thus depressed the wages of the American migrants.

Acting in concert, they wield political power, too. In 1962, the government sought to come to the defense of the American migrant by requiring growers to offer a minimum hourly wage—95 cents an hour—before seeking foreign labor. The growers were not alone or voiceless. Acting together, they contacted the Florida senators; the senators contacted the White House. The White House responded by

ordering the suspension of the 95-cent order. Result: the field workers of Florida were sentenced to another season of near-starvation wages.

Many and potent were the voices protesting the threat of grower hardship or bankruptcy should they be required to pay 95 cents an hour (all of $38 dollars for a forty-hour week). But who among the migrants could go to Washington to protest not the threat but the persistent and painful *fact* of hardship and bankruptcy among the workers?

Nearly everyone has a lobbyist (a "spokesman," if you prefer euphemisms) in Washington. The potash makers, as a case in point, have the American Potash Institute. Even wild animals and migrant birds are represented (the National Wildlife Federation boasts one of the handsomer buildings in Washington). A lobbyist for migrant birds, but none for migrant human beings.* Who ever heard of the poor hiring a lobbyist?

And how many migrant workers, how many stranded Kentucky coal miners, how many slum dwellers could ever manage to appear on the list of financial contributors to a congressman's or senator's political campaign?

For decades, slum tenants have suffered rats, filth, leaks, standing water, broken windows, faulty plumbing and wiring—blatant violations not only of standards of safety and human self-respect but of local housing laws as well. But in city after city, year after year, tenants suffered these torments and dangers singly and helplessly, while in city after city, year after year, the landlords, more affluent and powerful, successfully thwarted effective enforcement of the law.

Of all the afflictions of the poor, perhaps the harshest is their aloneness.

* See note p. 179

Even the man in the next chair is out of reach.

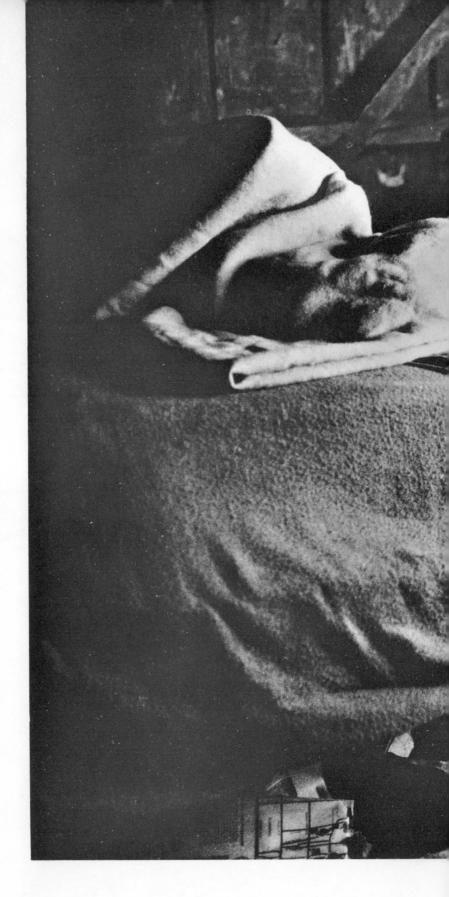

portfolio:

the children

of poverty

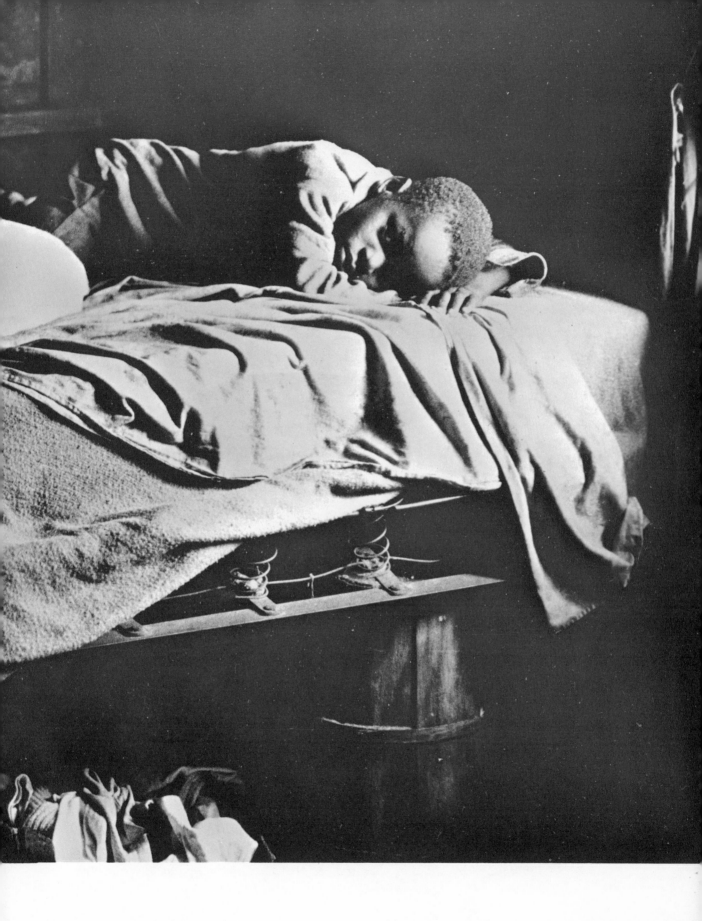

The greatest imperative is that attention be paid to poverty's children.
For without such attention, without heroic efforts to rescue them from
ignorance and squalor, they will be the poor of tomorrow, the burden
of tomorrow, the shame of tomorrow.

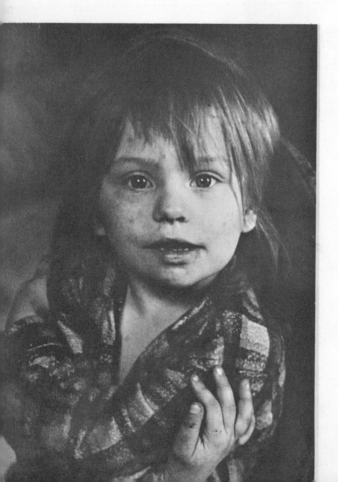

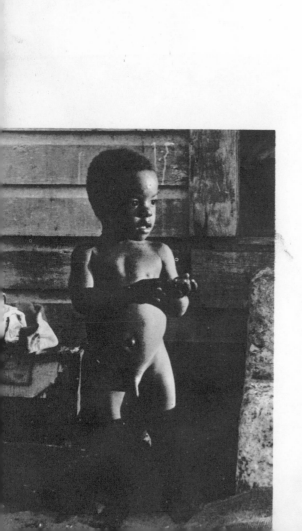

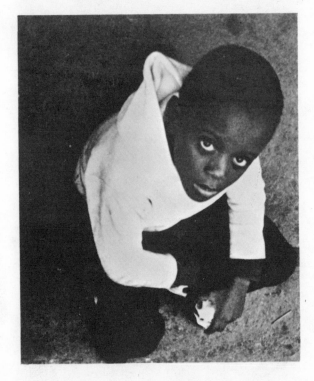

conclusion

Esther Cook, migrant mother making sixty cents a hamper picking beans . . . Darell Graves and Ray Newton, exiles, trapped in a society on the dole . . . John Patterson, struggling to coax a living from the sandy Arkansas soil . . . Four sisters in Chicago, the mothers as well as the children of fatherless families . . . The Ross family, spending Christmas in a basement furnace room . . . Alice Randall, fighting a losing battle with city hall . . . John Wilson, dishwasher, too poor to be helped . . . Roberta Clark, serving out a life sentence in a "hotel," in the core of Chicago's slums.

THESE are America's dispossessed.

The question is; How are they to be "repossessed"?

A beginning has been made. War has been declared on American poverty. The poor have now been granted official recognition by the United States government.

That fact is of cardinal importance. With the existence of massive poverty in America publicly as well as officially recognized and discussed, the amount of energy, talent, attention and funds devoted to the problem has multiplied manyfold.

The main thrust of the anti-poverty program is the education and training of the poor. A substantial effort is being made through President Johnson's education proposals as well as through the War on Poverty, to rectify the present imbalance of the public school system, under which the least resources have gone where the teaching job is toughest.

Book learning and vocational skills are indispensable if the bonds of poverty are to be broken. But there is another ingredient that could be even more important, even more precious to the poor: a voice of their own—the power to speak and be heard. Until this comes to pass, the poor will continue to exist largely at the sufferance of the rest of society, receiving only such benefits and aid as others deign to give them.

The education of the poor must extend beyond the three R's. Vital lessons for the poor have been written in the notebooks of the American civil rights movement: that the lot of even the most lowly and most abused is not immutable, is not decreed for all time, does not have to be suffered in silence. It *can* be changed, and effective protest is the agent of change.

These lessons have yet to be absorbed by the poor. It is no accident that the Washington, D. C. school with but one basin for 260 children as well as the antiquated overcrowded school with converted locker rooms for class rooms (p. 127) are both located in slum areas. Nor is it an accident that there are no such schools in the affluent areas of the city. Parents well-educated in good schools are not only more aware of and concerned with the school lives of their children; they also know that school buildings need *not* be dilapidated, ill-equipped and overcrowded, that protests properly lodged will bring about improvement. And they know *how* to protest. Much of this knowledge has never come to slum parents, themselves poorly educated in poor rural or slum schools.

It is no accident that due to inadequate medical staff, indigent patients are obliged to wait three, six, sometimes even twelve hours to see a doctor in the Emergency Room of Washington, D. C.'s General Hospital. They are accustomed to such waits; they have never known anything different. Even if they believed things could be better, to whom would they protest? And who would listen?

And so they wait—and suffer—in silence.

166

In his struggle for his civil rights, the American Negro has discovered that it is not necessary to suffer in silence. With a cause, with leaders, with tried and proven techniques of protest, he speaks now, and he is heard—he is listened to.

America's poor are surely not lacking in causes, injustices and wrongs. There are the nocturnal invasions of homes by welfare investigators (more to be expected of totalitarian Russia than of democratic America); pregnant girls forced to induce "winos" to claim paternity of their unborn child; children vomiting in school from malnutrition. These, and many more. But these are wrongs and injustices of which most Americans are unaware. Like many of the massive discriminations against the Southern Negro through the first half of this century, they are beneath the line of public visibility. They have yet to prick the American conscience.

No, the poor do not lack for causes. But they have yet to find the leaders, yet to learn the techniques of protest.

The civil rights movement has drawn much of its public sympathy because of the patent injustice of dooming a man to a lifetime of discrimination the very instant he is born—born with a black skin he did not choose and cannot shed for as long as he lives, no matter how noble his effort or how brilliant his achievement.

The poor do not *visibly* suffer this same injustice. They may be born poor, but the American dream and the Horatio Alger legend have it that in this land of opportunity, there is no limit to the heights a man can·reach—any man, no matter how humble his origins—*if he will but try*. In the standard man-in-the-street interpretation of the American dream, it is lack of initiative—laziness, to put it bluntly —that makes the poor poor and keeps them that way.

But the American dream deserves a closer, more critical look. Many, if not most, of the American poor—white *and* black—are, like the Negro, doomed the instant they are born, destined for a life of ignorance, squalor and perpetuated poverty—*unless* society intervenes to break the chain.

If, for example, you are born of an unmarried welfare mother in the heart of city blight, you are destined to go to a slum school where the buildings are the shabbiest, the play space the skimpiest, the text books the remotest from your life, your interests, your experience . . . destined to grow up in a slum where *no* man has a good job, where, in fact, one man in four has no job at all (So what's the use? Why stay in school when life is so much more exciting on the outside?) . . . destined to grow up with a gang of goal-less kids who have little hope of making an *honest* living, so they resort to the next best thing . . .

Or if you're born the child of a migrant mother and father, you are doomed from birth to a wandering life with no steady home, no steady friends, no steady job for father; to a life where school itself is almost a "frill."

Yes, such persons *can* break out of their past, their environment. The rags-to-riches stories prove it.

(But for each rags-to-riches story, how many hundreds of thousands, how many million rags-to-*rags* stories are there? And if for those born in poverty—whether white *or* black—the chances of escape are but one in a thousand, or one in ten thousand, then their poverty is virtually as unshedable as the Negro's black skin.)

The civil rights won by the American Negro have not all been gained by sit-ins and protest marches. They have been won in the courtroom as well.

The poor can also profit by making the law their ally, by learning what few of them realize: that they have rights; that life is not just an array of privileges which society bestows upon them at its whim and discretion. It may come as a surprise to the poor, and a shock to others, to discover, for example, that the granting or denial of welfare assistance is not a divine right of welfare departments; that the decision of a welfare worker to deny aid to a Puerto Rican mother and her children can be (and was) challenged in the courts —and reversed! Or that the nocturnal invasions of homes is likewise not a divine right of investigators and that a government anti-poverty official can be (and was) summoned in the middle of the

168

night to censure the investigator. Or that laws such as Florida's (p. 120) providing ceilings on welfare grants regardless of family size may be (and were) challenged in the courts and ruled unconstitutional—just as many long-standing anti-Negro laws have been challenged and struck down by the courts.

In sum, the education of the poor should not stop with the three Rs. It should include a fourth R: Rights—the right to challenge, the right to insist on change.

No one should yield to the tempting thought that it will be possible to take the experience and lessons of the American civil rights movement and transfer them, intact, to a putative "poverty movement." The Negroes are homogeneous, set apart from the rest of society by one common and unmistakable characteristic. They speak a common language. The poor are not one: they are many— white and black, Puerto Rican and Irish, Italian and Mexican. They are migrant farm worker and dishwasher; ex-miner and ex-handyman. Frequently, they have no use for one another. No one should expect, therefore, the blossoming of a national "poverty movement," the natural counterpart of the civil rights movement.

Nor will finding the leaders of protest from among the poor be any simple matter. It is tempting to sentimentalize about the poor, to overestimate their endowments, to picture them simply as a downtrodden, put-upon mass of people bubbling not only with unrest but with untapped resources, merely waiting for the Messiah among them to help them rise up. But in our unusually (almost uniquely) open society, where talent is extraordinarily free to find its way upward, the poor are naturally overweighted with the less talented, the less ambitious, and leaders are scarce. On the other hand, four decades ago, perhaps even two, the same was doubtless said of the American Negro; yet leaders have emerged. If a purposeful search is made for leaders among the poor, if a purposeful effort is made to develop their full potential, who is to say there are none to be found?

In any event, the effort must be made. The development among the poor of leaders of protest, and the education of the poor to the *techniques* of protest are among the most vital steps to progress, for protest will arouse the American conscience and shape the national will. And whatever a nation *wills* to do, it can do.

Consider England. Her wealth is small compared with that of the United States (her *total* output is less than the mere *increase* in American output in a three-year period). Yet it has been observed that "there is nothing in Great Britain comparable to the squalor and despair of the vast urban slums and rural wastelands of the United States." This is no accident. It is the result of deliberate policies, of the determination of a nation not to tolerate mass poverty.

In France, it is said to be difficult to find a very large family that is also very poor. This, too, results from an act of national will: the family allowance plan that gives all families a minimum per-child living allowance. In America, by contrast, it is difficult to find, among the less skilled, a very large family that is not also a very poor family.

Both these countries, like most of Europe, have been far more preoccupied with providing adequate *floors* under their economies than America, which has been more concerned with raising the ceiling of limits to which the successful can rise, and which has allowed the floors to fall into disrepair.

The United States has now declared war on its poverty, but, as the warriors themselves would acknowledge, that is only *part* of the agenda of bringing the poor back into the mainstream of progress. Acts of national will could fill in the gaps, and could come to the aid of dispossessed Americans such as you have met in this book. Acts of national will could, for example, provide a livable minimum wage for John Wilson, dishwasher; could give Esther Cook, American migrant, the same protections enjoyed by the non-citizens in the next field; could take the initiative in helping Lucille Campbell avoid unwanted children; could replace ancient school buildings and pay teachers a respectable salary; could do vastly more to teach and re-habilitate society's dependents and help them get *off* the welfare rolls; could provide a proper, not a pauper's, living for the old, the dependent young, the jobless; could rescue the Rosses from their basement furnace room and the Alice Randalls and the Roberta Clarks from their imprisonment in slum squalor—not with massive piles of brick of an "Early Penitentiary" mode of design, but with attractively designed housing, with provision for leisure, culture, recreation.

Can't afford it? Too expensive?

Nonsense. America can afford to do whatever it makes up its mind to do. Even fly to the moon.

But new laws and added dollars are not the only weapons in the War on Poverty. Often the warmth of a friendly voice or the sight of a patient, outreaching hand can do the work of millions. In the War on Poverty, those voices and hands are most likely to belong to the "domestic Peace Corps" volunteers, the Affluent Society's roving ambassadors to the poor, together with lay persons—housewives, lawyers, teenagers, what-will-you, who may become part-time enlistees in this new war. Collectively, these Samaritans who are willing to work or live *among* the poor could become the most important asset in the War on Poverty, for its success will depend in large measure on whether it turns out to be a headquarters war or a neighborhood war; a desk-bound war or a shoe-leather war; exclusively a big-city war or also a "creeks and hollers" war. For Darell Graves, the ex-coal miner who needs retraining, for example, the training center 45 miles away is useless; it might as well be in a different country. Unless training centers and other facilities are brought to the small town near Darell, and to other small towns like it, Darell and others like him will be by-passed by the War on Poverty.

But you don't have to live in the hills of Kentucky to be isolated. To many of those serving out a life sentence in the slums, a three-transfer bus trip across town to a health center or training school or birth control clinic may be just as arduous (or frightening) as the ten-mile trip to town for Darell Graves.

So help, if it is to be effective, must not be a distant thing. It must reach out to the poor. It must be a neighborhood affair.

America is a work-worshipping country. Work is a cardinal virtue, idleness a cardinal sin. Many, for example, share the vigorous view of the Kentucky lawyer (p. 28) that people should work for their welfare grants. It matters not whether the work is useful or instructive. Work is a virtue, idleness a sin.

But why not shift the emphasis? Why not promote *learning* to head the list of American virtues and make ignorance a paramount sin? If, for instance, welfare recipients are to be forced to some activity, why not let it be a course of instruction, whether it be reading and writing, or a skill or trade, or simply childraising and homemaking? And why not remove every obstacle to the fullest enjoyment of this new-found cardinal virtue? Why not revive the principle of the GI Bill of Rights, for *every* American who is capable of and interested in, but is barred financially from, the further pursuit of knowledge? And why not pay subsistence grants to high school students like ghetto-trapped John Ash (p. 85), who otherwise would be obliged to quit school and go to work.

The war on poverty will be no one-year skirmish. American poverty is deep-rooted. The residue of decades of neglect will not be quickly erased.

But this does not justify despair. There is despair enough among the poor. Of course the poor have always been with us, but need they always be? Medical science has yet to find a cure for cancer, but the search goes on. Who is to say there is no remedy for the cancer of poverty?

Other countries have, in fact, largely won their struggles with mass poverty. In the Atlantic world, America is said to be one of the last industrial democracies to retain massive poverty. If others can eliminate it, why not the United States?

Yes, why not? Twenty-four years ago, America joined the war against Fascism, quadrupled its budget, spent a third of a *trillion* dollars fighting a global war, worked, sacrificed—and won. Who is to say such a nation cannot win this new war—if it wills to do so?

And who is to say that a nation determined to spare no effort or expense to put a man on the moon is incapable of equal dedication to a mission of human rescue, incapable of making life not merely livable but palatable for millions of impoverished human beings who are destined to remain earthbound?

It comes down to a matter of will, or priorities, of effort.

We come full circle, to the words of Pericles:

> ". . . poverty we think it no disgrace to acknowledge, but a real degradation to make no effort to overcome."

notes and sources

ABBREVIATIONS USED

Bagdikian: Ben H. Bagdikian, *In the Midst of Plenty*, Beacon Press, 1964.

Cong. Rec.: Congressional Record.

Greenleigh: "Facts, Fallacies and Future: A Study of the Aid to Dependent Children Program of Cook County, Illinois," by Arthur Greenleigh Associates, Inc., 1960.

HEW: Department of Health, Education and Welfare.

May: Edgar May, *The Wasted Americans*, Harper and Row, 1964.

PAGE

INTRODUCTION

1   *Rat bites in New York, Washington:* New York Health Department; Washington *Daily News,* January 28, 1965.

1   *32 cents a day for Mississippi children:* Social Security Bulletin, April, 1964, p. 42.

2   *D. C. food allowance 17½ cents per meal:* D. C. Department of Welfare, Sample Grants Based on Maximum Shelter Allowance Without Income. Under this schedule, a family of 12 receives about $189 per month to feed 12 people approximately 90 meals per month each.

2   *U. S. spends more on migrant birds than on migrant human beings:* in FY 1964, the U. S. Fish and Wildlife Service says $35.6 million was spent on migrant birds. In that same year, although there were other U. S. programs that affected migrant workers indirectly, the only one that can be separately

identified as exclusively for the welfare of migrant workers is $2 million appropriated under the Migrant Health Act. See Report to the Senate Subcommittee on Migratory Labor by HEW, June 1964, p. 5.

3   *Average jobless benefit $35 per week:* Bureau of Employment Security, U. S. Department of Labor.

3   *Average social security benefit $29 per week:* Social Security Administration monthly fact sheet, January 26, 1965.

3   *Mal-education in South Chicago slum:* May, 73.

3   *A small fraction of public housing program a reality:* The Housing Act of 1949 authorized 810,000 public housing units. As of January, 1965, only 459,000 of these had been built. Even if the Johnson housing goals are fully realized, less than 700,000 units will have been built by 1969—twenty years after the 1949 Act.

3   *Public housing will only house one slum family in eighty:* Andrew Hacker, New York *Times Magazine*, March 22, 1964.

THE DISPOSSESSED

8   *Half a million children still work in the fields: injuries to California farm children:* Bagdikian, 113.

11   *Migrant works 109 days a year:* Senate Report 167, 88th Congress, 1st Session (1963), p. 1.

11   *Farm accident rate third highest: Accident Facts, 1964,* National Safety Council, Chicago.

16   *Exclusion of migrants from social insurance laws:* Department of Labor. Those not covered by the minimum wage law include many self-employed and many whose jobs are essentially intra-state in nature and thus might not be reachable under Federal law.

THE EXILES

23   *". . . deserted by their union . . .":* United Mine Worker members in Appalachia are bitter over the fact that, due to the sickness of the coal industry, the decline of unionism in the mines, the failure of coal operators to pay into the pension trust fund and the consequent depletion of that fund, the union has withdrawn hospitalization benefits from thousands of ex-miners, benefits which the miners had counted on. One miner recounted how he had received a curt form letter from the union advising him that, despite his 35 years in union mines, he was no longer eligible for hospital and health benefits— because he had been unemployed for more than a year.

24   *"Nobody could bring themselves to provide work":* As of early 1965, a works program for unemployed fathers of dependent children had been begun in Eastern Kentucky.

THE EXILES THROUGH AFFLUENT EYES

26   *Letcher County statistics:* U. S. Census Bureau; Kentucky Bureau of Employment Security; U. S. Department of Health, Education and Welfare.

FARMER

31, 34   *Statistics re cotton subsidies to small and large farmers:* 109 Cong. Rec. 21967-21970 (daily). The cotton subsidy is now 6½ instead of 8½ cents.

35–7   *Funds for price supports versus FHA operating loans:* FY 1966, Budget Appendix, p. 147 (price support cost, FY 1964: $3.2 billion); p. 177 (FHA operating loans: $298 million).

37   *One-twenty-fifth as much for housing loans:* FY 1966 Budget Appendix, p. 172. Housing grants were eliminated in the FY 1965 Appropriation Act.

37   *Rural renewal funds:* FY 1966 Budget Appendix, p. 174.

39   *Some in Congress labeled the plan 'Communistic':* 110 Cong. Rec. 16195 (daily), July 23, 1964.

THE UNWANTED

57   *Birth-rate as high as in India:* Planned Parenthood Association of Chicago *"Problems of Bearing and Rearing Children in High Fertility, Low Income, Low Education American Families."*

57   *Each unwanted child costs $13,000; birth control services cost $30 a year:* Cook County School System; Planned Parenthood Association, Chicago.

57   *Cook County ADC expenditures:* figures presented by Illinois Public Aid Director Harold Swank, 1964.

THE SAMARITAN AS COP

73   *Three a.m. investigator intrusion:* Greenleigh, 67.

75   *James Henry incident:* Greenleigh, 18.

75–6   *Examples of welfare-check deductions:* Greenleigh, Associates, Inc., 1964 Report on Public Welfare in the State of Washington, pp. V-20-21.

77   *Case worker has 138 other clients:* Edgar May cites the monthly average case load in Erie County, N. Y., at 139; but he also cites the average case load in Texas at 333, in Alabama at 315; in Mississippi at 216. May, 112.

77   *175 varieties of welfare forms:* Greenleigh, 68.

79   *Alabama and New York welfare grants:* Social Security Bulletin, April 1964, p. 42.

80   *Cotton subsidies:* 109 Congressional Record 21967-21970 (daily), 1953.

A PLEA FOR AN END TO TONGUE-CLUCKING

83   *Quote, "If a man has anything,"* etc.: From Washington *Post,* January 12, 1964.

YOU CAN'T FIGHT CITY HALL

105   *Alice Randall case true in every detail:* This is taken from an actual case presented to Mayor Wagner in 1963 by WMCA Women's Call for Action group in New York City, whose cooperation is hereby gratefully acknowledged.

105   *18 Water complaints to four departments:* In early 1965, due principally to the Women's Call for Action efforts, New York City inaugurated a single telephone number for the receipt of all housing complaints. This is not, however, true of other cities. The jurisdictional squabble over the rat bite is from May.

105   *1.5 million homes built in 1964, less than 1.5 percent public housing:* President's Economic Report, January, 1965, p. 235.

105   *On 25th anniversary, less than one percent public housing:* May, 134.

"WE CAN'T HELP HIM—HE'S TOO POOR"

106–7   *John Wilson incident:* Washington *Post:* February 17, 1964.

NO HIDIN' PLACE

111   *$3600 cost of keeping a child in institution:* This is the cost of keeping a child in Washington, D. C.'s Junior Village. Washington *Post,* February 13, 1965.

IMBALANCE

119   *1963 Federal highway versus public housing expenditures:* FY 1966 Budget Appendix, page 260; FY 1966 Budget, p. 306.

176

WHOSE WELFARE STATE?

120 *Mississippi Welfare allowances:* Social Security Bulletin, April, 1964, p. 42.

120 *Florida welfare allowances:* May, 56.

120 *Chicago clothing allowances:* Greenleigh, 42.

120 *Welfare allowances one dollar per day:* HEW Statistics on Public Assistance, December, 1964.

122 *Tax subsidies to various oil companies:* 110 Cong. Rec. 2103 (daily), 1964. Tax subsidy computed by comparing tax actually paid by these corporations with what they would have paid at the then-existing 52 percent corporate rate.

123–4 *Maximum jobless benefits in Alabama; average benefits in U. S.:* Significant Provisions of State Unemployment Insurance Laws, U. S. Department of Labor, January 1, 1965; U. S. Department of Labor Annual Report, 1964.

123 *Average social security payment:* HEW, *Current Social Security Operations*, January 26, 1965.

124 *Postal subsidies to magazines:* Government Subsidy Historical Review, House Agriculture Committee (Revised May 10, 1960), p. 5.

125 *Housing statistics:* President's Economic Report, January 1964, p. 252; Andrew Hacker, New York *Times Magazine*, March 22, 1964; FY 1965 Budget, p. 286.

125 *Shipbuilding subsidies:* 1963 Annual Report of U. S. Maritime Commission, p. 4.

125 *D. C. Welfare allowances:* See note, p. 2.

125 *Cotton subsidies:* 109 Cong. Rec. 21967-21970 (daily), December 3, 1963.

"BUT WE CAN'T AFFORD TO HELP THE POOR"

126 *Space appropriations carried overwhelmingly:* Appropriations passed by voice vote in Senate (June 28, 1961); passed 354-59 in House (July 20, 1961).

126 *Cost of staffing Emergency Room:* D. C. General Hospital.

126–7 *Military Construction vote:* May 29, 1964; From Congressional Quarterly, p. 1034.

127 *Washington, D. C. Playground closing:* Washington *Post*, March 1, 1965.

127 *Rivers and Harbors votes:* 1962 Congressional Quarterly Almanac, p. 457.

127 *Ludlow, Harrison, Shaw schools:* D. C. School System.

128 *Post-Berlin budget increase and reaction:* Pres. Kennedy speech, July 25, 1961; New York *Times*, July 27, 28 and 30, 1961.

129   *Military pay increases:* Department of Defense. Increases were voted in 1952, 1955, 1958, 1963 and 1964. Votes are on $1.2 billion increase in 1963. Congressional Quarterly Almanac, 1963, p. 447.

129   *Perry County school statistics:* Perry County School System.

THE PRICE OF OUR FAILURES

130   *Blight in New York City:* Harlem Youth Opportunities Unlimited, Inc., *Youth in the Ghetto,* 1964, pp. 137-61.

130   *Blight in Sacramento, Los Angeles:* Conference on Economic Progress, *Poverty and Deprivation in the U. S.,* 1962, p. 69.

131   *Blight in Newark:* Housing Authority of the City of Newark, *The Cost of Slums in Newark,* 1946, p. 14.

131   *Draftee statistics:* The President's Task Force on Manpower Conservation, *One Third of A Nation,* January 1, 1964.

131   *Average dope addict must beg, borrow or steal $50,000:* Mayor Wagner has told Labor Department officials that a dope addict must steal roughly $50,000 worth of property in order to "fence" it and net enough cash to feed his habit and support himself.

131   *Case loads of social workers:* May, 112.

131   *Increase in welfare costs: Source of Funds Expended for Public Assistance Payments,* Fiscal Year ended June 30, 1964 and Fiscal Year ended June 30, 1954 Bureau of Family Services, Welfare Administration, U. S. Department of Health, Education & Welfare.

131   *Birth control costs; costs of unwanted children:* See note on p. 57, above.

132   *Costs of children on welfare, foster homes, institutions: Advance Release of Statistics on Public Assistance,* June 1964, Bureau of Family Services, Welfare Administration, U. S. Department Health, Education & Welfare.

HURDLES

137   *Willie Johnson story:* Bagdikian, 49.

140–1   *Rent differences for whites and Negroes:* Buffalo—May, 132: Chicago—Greenleigh, 54.

143   *Educational deficiencies of South Chicagoans:* May, 73.

143   *State per-child school expenditures:* 1964 Statistical Abstract of the U. S., p. 126.

143   *Half as much spent on schools in slums as suburbs:* James B. Conant, *Slums and Suburbs,* p. 3.

143   *Half heads of household had less than eighth grade Education:* Conference on Economic Progress, *Poverty and Deprivation in the U. S.,* p. 71.

144   *$53 in unemployment compensation:* This is the maximum for the District of Columbia; Source: U. S. Employment Service.

146   *Arlington and Perry County family income:* Standard Rate and Data Market Guide.

146   *Perry County unemployment, welfare:* U. S. Department of Labor: Kentucky Department of Employment Security.

146–7   *Arlington versus Perry County and D. C. School statistics:* Figures obtained from the respective school systems. Arlington versus D. C. elementary school per-pupil expenditures: $580 vs. $312.

153   *No lobbyist for migrant human beings:* There are, however, many church, labor and other civic organizations both in Washington and around the country who have worked actively and often effectively on the migrants' behalf. For example, it was their persistent pressure on Congress over many years that resulted in an end to the "bracero" program in 1964.

CONCLUSION

168   *Decision of welfare worker to deny aid challenged:* For examples of questions susceptible to legal challenge, see various papers presented at HEW Conference on the Extension of Legal Services to the Poor (Washington, Nov. 12-14, 1964), especially Edward Sparer, "The New Public Law."

169   *Challenge of maximum welfare grants:* Collins v. State Board of Welfare, 81 NW 2nd 4 (1957).

170   *Description of England's poverty:* French family allowances; U. S. last Atlantic democracy with mass poverty: Daniel Patrick Moynihan, "Religion, Race and the War on Poverty," *The Harvard Review*, Spring, 1964.

171–2   *Suggestions for promoting learning:* the War on Poverty and other existing legislation already contains the seeds of some of these ideas (e.g., some 32,000 unemployed parents on welfare are in various courses of training).

photographic notes

Equipment: All pictures in this book were taken with a Nikon F, with 28, 50 and 105 mm. Nikor lenses and a 300 mm. f/5.6 Rokunar lens. No filters were used. The most useful lenses were the 28 mm. (virtually all the interior shots required the 28 mm. lens) and the 300 mm. lens which made it possible to get candid unposed facial studies from long distances. The 300 mm. Rokunar is both extremely sharp and extremely light, and therefore unusually easy to handle for such a long lens.

Film: Tri-X film was used throughout. Its flexibility is remarkable: on the same roll of film, I took outdoor shots in the bright Arizona sun (at 1/1000 second) and very dark interiors in dimly lit slum houses or shacks at 1/5 second and got fine negatives in both cases.

Flash equipment: None. All pictures were taken in available light, with the camera hand-held, at speeds as slow as 1/2 second, holding my breath and using arm and shoulder as a tripod.

Light meter: None. I feel a light meter gets between the photographer and his subject and interferes with that one instant that can never be recaptured.

Developing: Aga-fine film developer used throughout, developing by visual inspection, and supplementing the Aga-fine by popping the film in Dektol paper developer for an instant to give the negatives extra punch.

Enlarging: Almost no cropping was done in the dark room. I try, as much as I can, to frame the picture I want while I am taking it, by changing lenses.

George de Vincent

acknowledgments

THANKS beyond expression go to the many, many people both in Washington and throughout the country who gave generously and unstintingly of their time to help open doors to the homes and lives of the "dispossessed" Americans, among them the following: William and Marge Bell, Owen Biles, Melvin Brown, John Burton, John Byron, Harry and Anne Caudill, Lester Fox, Rita Freedman, Tom and Pat Gish, Herman Hankins, Robert Hankins, Rev. John Heine, Ray Hilliard, L. S. James, Willie Jones, Alice Kornegay, Clyde McGinnis, Saul Nimowitz, Grace Olivarez, Paul Piefer, Sal Ramirez, Emmett Roberts, Lyle Rogers, Edward Sparer, Carl Whitman, Sister Mary William, W. O. Wilson and Rev. J. S. Wright. If this book achieves our aim of opening other eyes besides our own to the life and lot of the American poor, those who helped us so greatly should know that it would not have been possible, but for their cooperation and generosity.

Grateful thanks, too, go to Hubert I. Bermont, whose help, advice —and friendship—have been invaluable; to Stefan Salter and Carol Michaels, for their patience, cheer, and graciousness in connection with the book's design; to Gertrude Callander, who stoically and efficiently bore the burden of the manuscript preparation; to Elizabeth Stern and Ann Allen, researchers extraordinary; to Arthur Greenleigh, to whose superb studies in the welfare field the public owes a deep debt of gratitude, and for whose advice and counsel this book owes a similar debt; and to Helen Hill Miller, whose unfailing patience in reading manuscripts in various states of dishevelment was surpassed only by the wisdom and helpfulness of her counsel.

Most of all we are indebted to our distinctly better halfs, Shelley and Leni, who were unfailingly patient and understanding during our travels among the "dispossessed," unfailingly reassuring when our spirits were low, and unfailingly tasteful and helpful both in appraising and improving the manuscript and in judging and helping to select the photographs. In short, the book profited from what and who they are, just as we do every day of our lives.

Philip M. Stern
George de Vincent